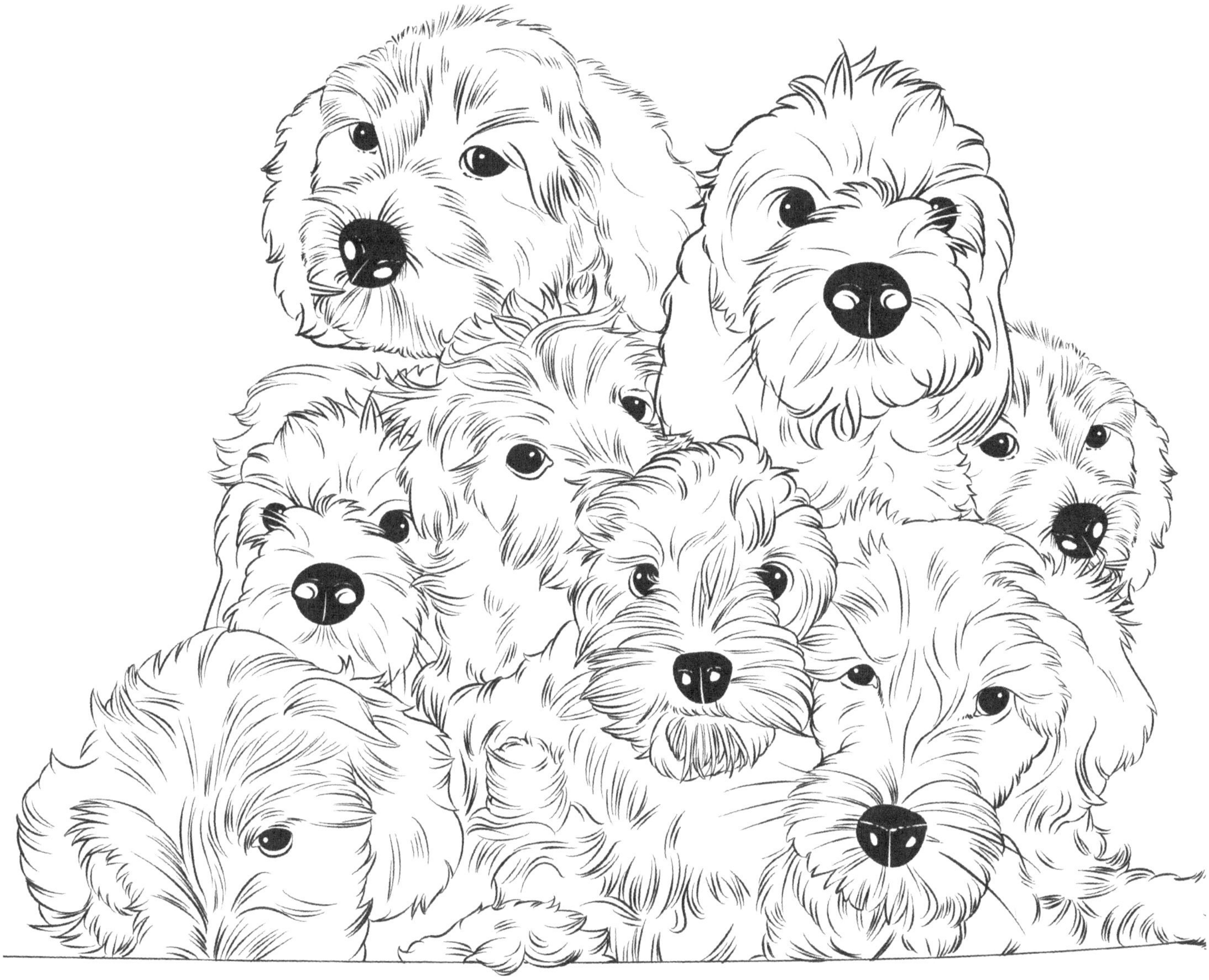

Little Labradoodle & Friends 🐾🐾

Doodle Lovers
Adult Coloring Book

Copyright ©2018 All rights reserved. Little Labradoodle Publishing, LLC 🐾 www.thelittlelabradoodle.com

Author: April M. Cox • Illustrator: Harry Aveira
Design & Layout by Nicole Lavoie of www.JustSayingDezigns.com

Copyright ©2018 All rights reserved.
No part of this book may be reproduced, distributed, or transmitted in any form or by any means, including photocopying, recording, or other electronic or mechanical methods, without the prior written permission of the publisher, except in the case of brief quotations embodied in critical reviews and certain other noncommercial uses permitted by copyright law.

Little Labradoodle Publishing, LLC
www.thelittlelabradoodle.com • info@thelittlelabradoodle.com

Second Edition: May, 2019 • ISBN 978-1-7324566-0-0

Welcome!

Join our mailing list at **www.thelittlelabradoodle.com/join**
to receive a **FREE** digital copy of this coloring book
so you can reprint your favorites.

Post photos of your completed pages online with
hash tag #thelittlelabradoodle or email us at:
contest@thelittlelabradoodle.com

We would love to feature your work and
you could win our monthly drawing!

Thank You!

- To my awesome illustrator, Harry Aveira
- To those who provided photos of fur babies
- To all those who are helping get the word out
  about The Little Labradoodle books.

Find us online at:
www.thelittlelabradoodle.com

Follow us on social media at:

- TheLittleLabradoodle
- TheLittleLabradoodle
- lil_labradoodle
- TheLittleLabradoodle

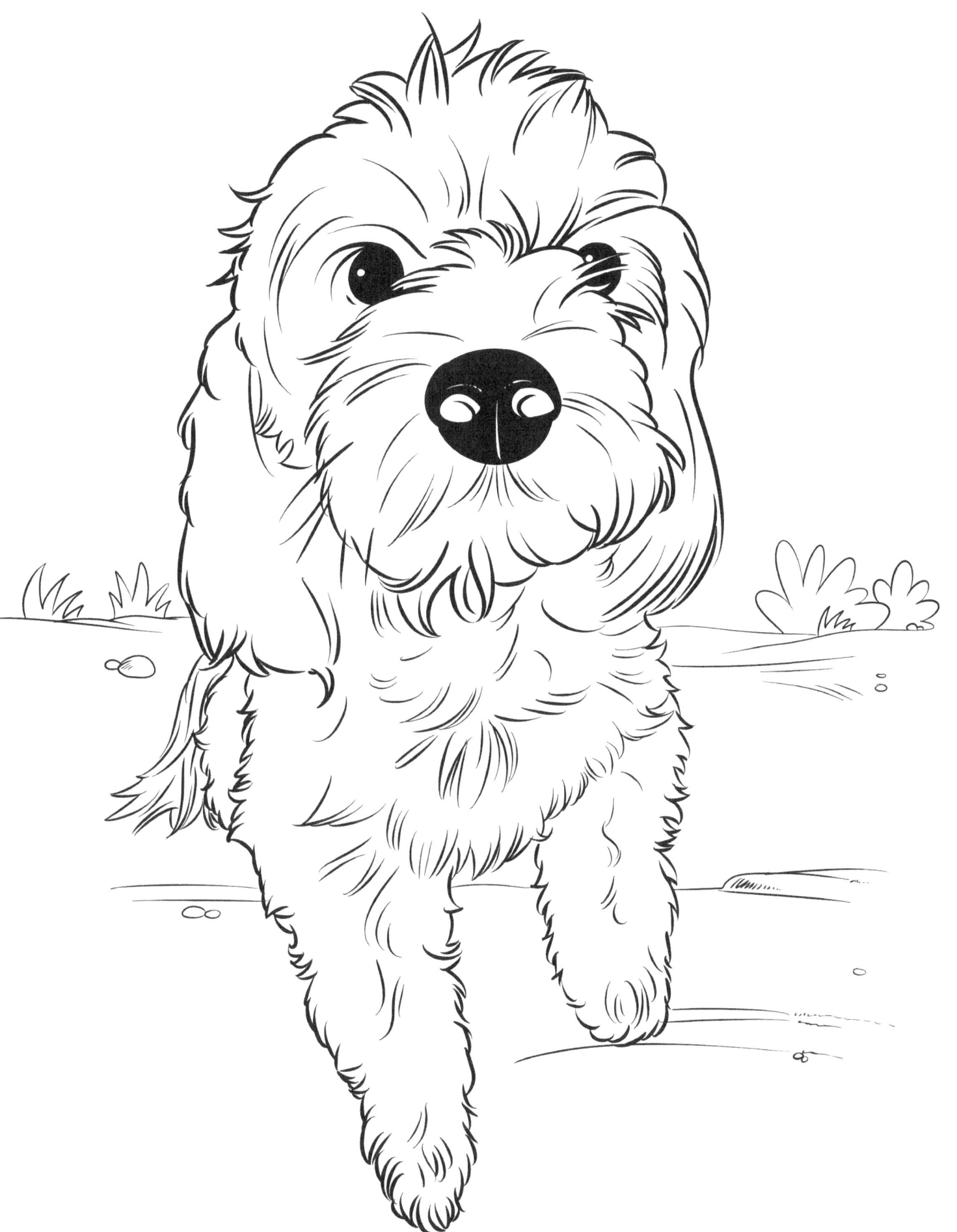

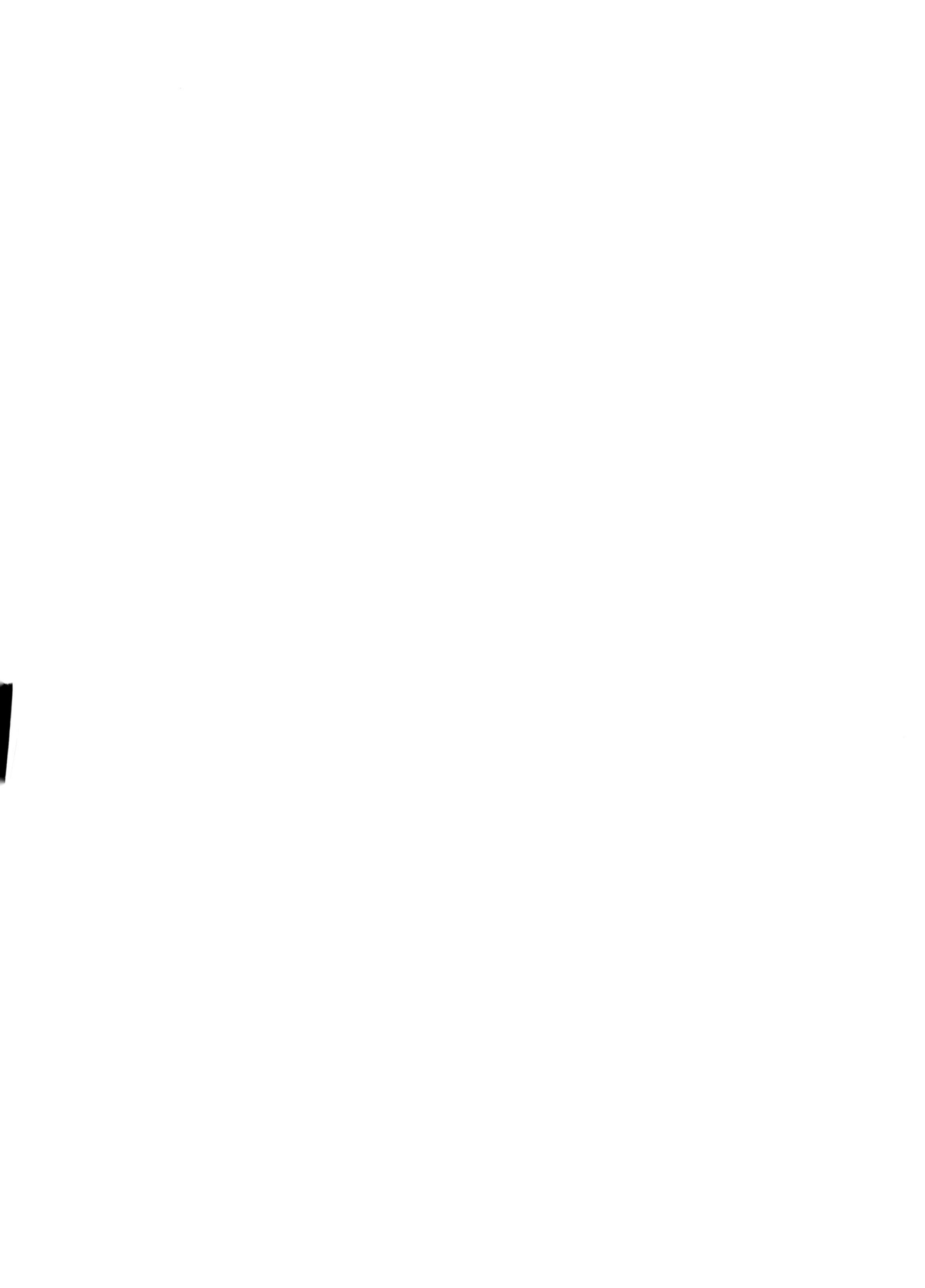

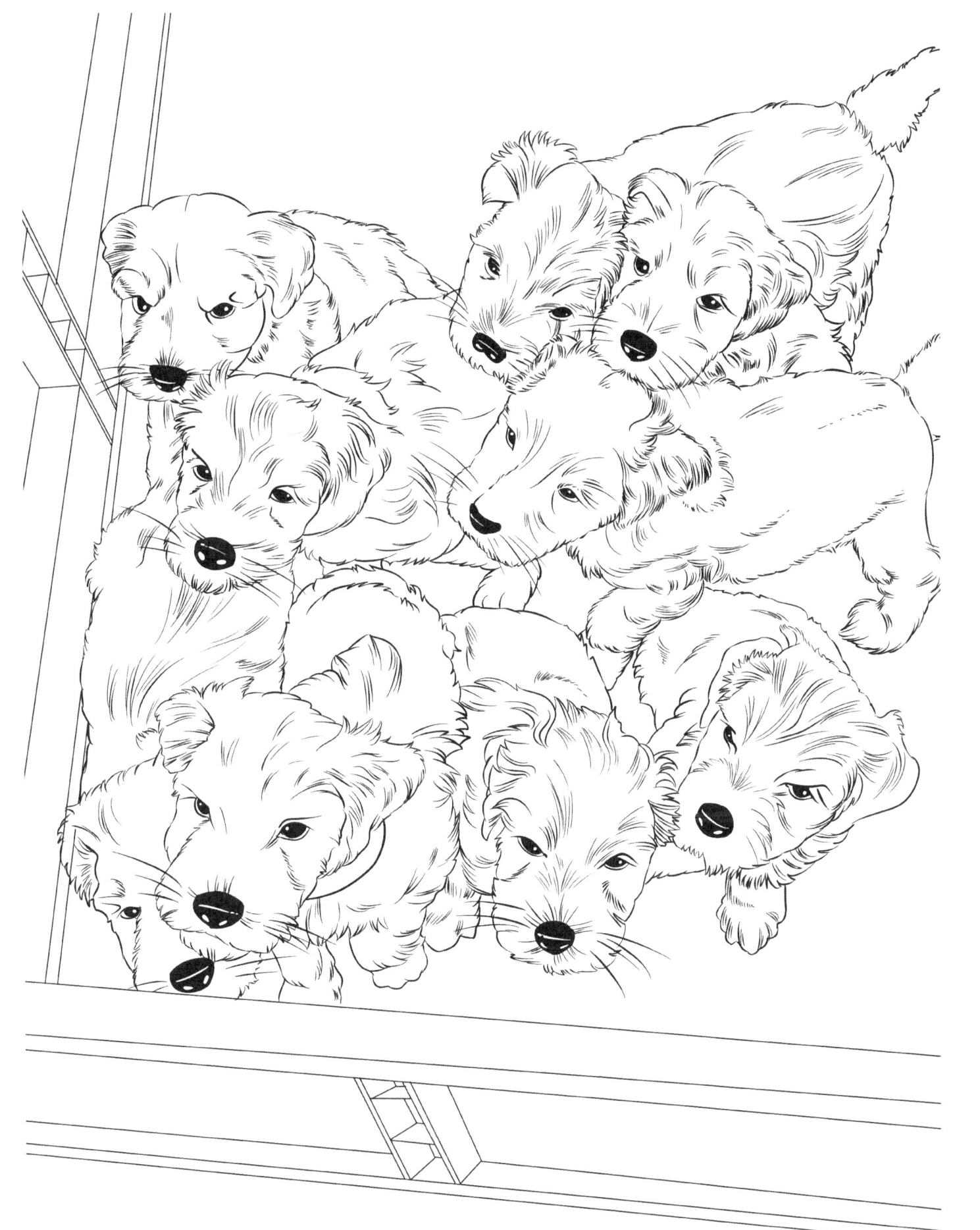

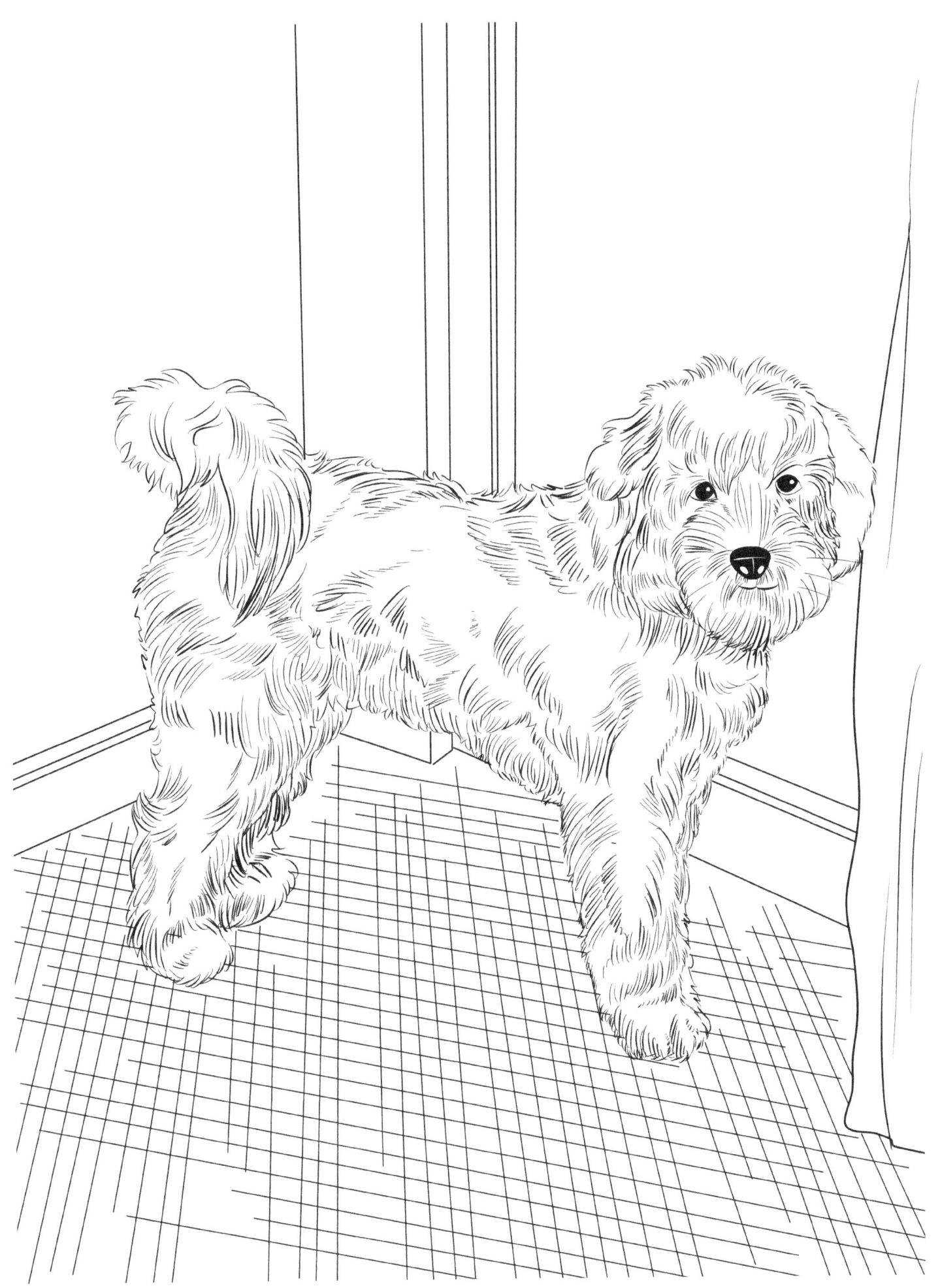

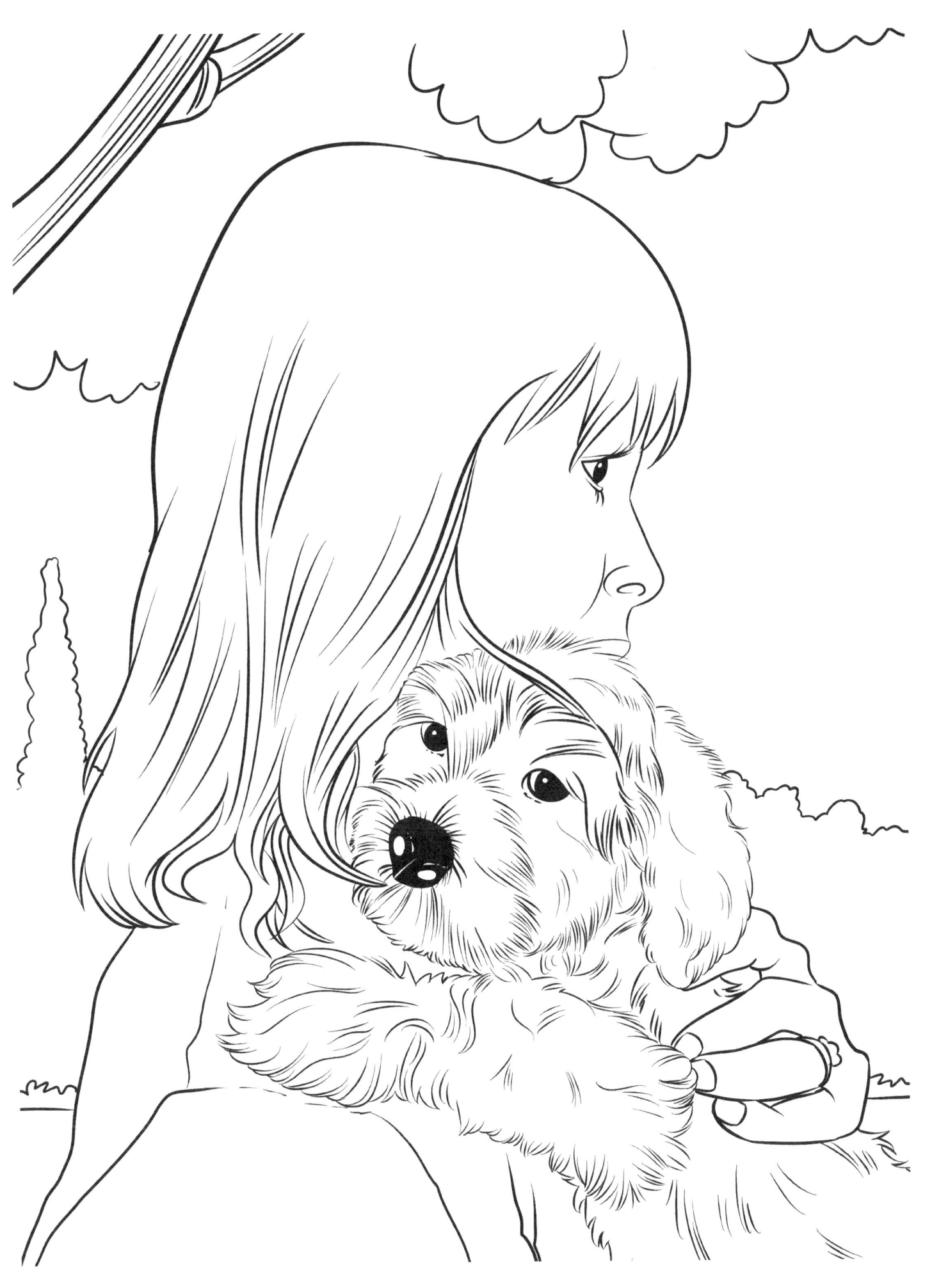

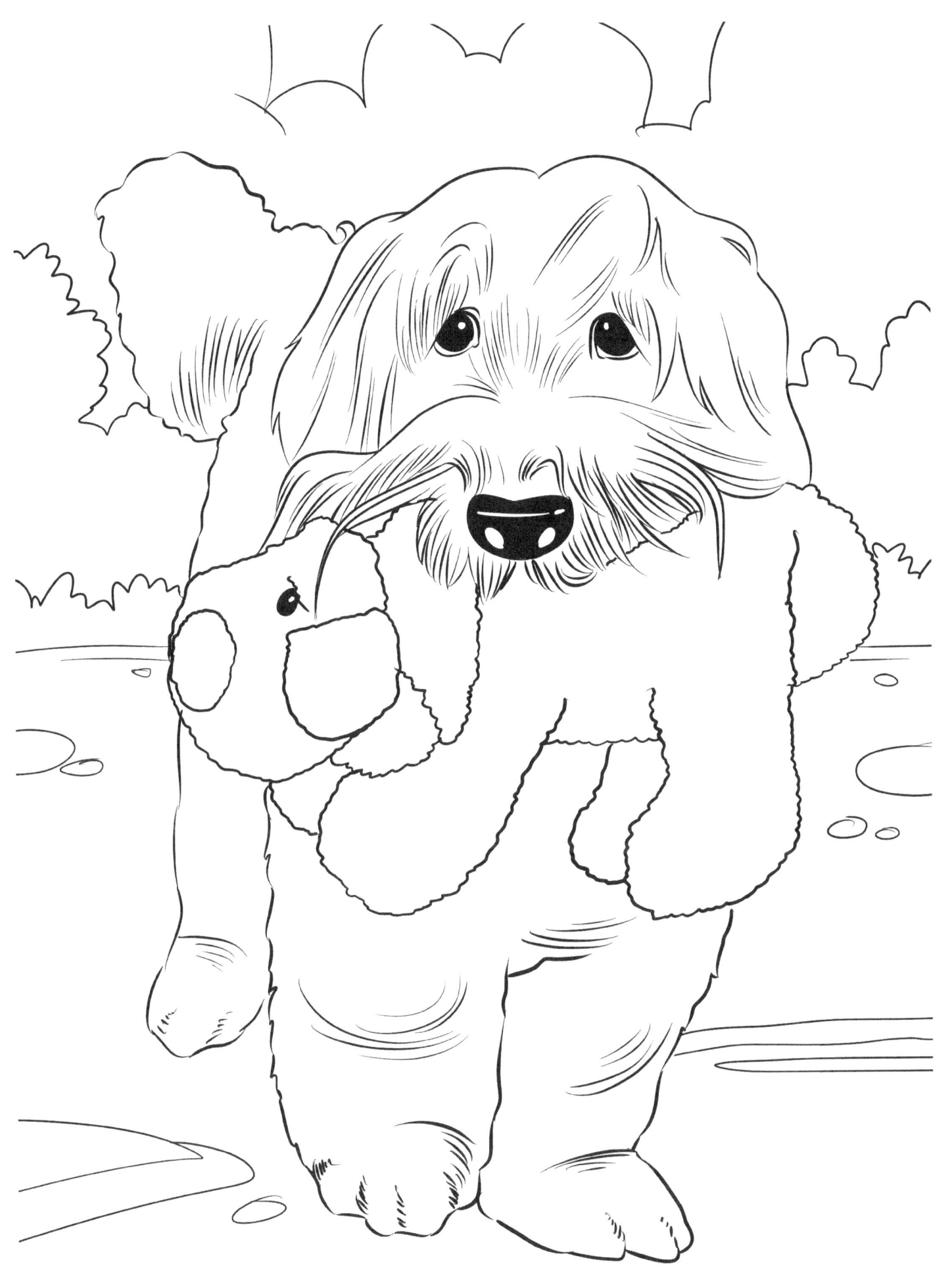

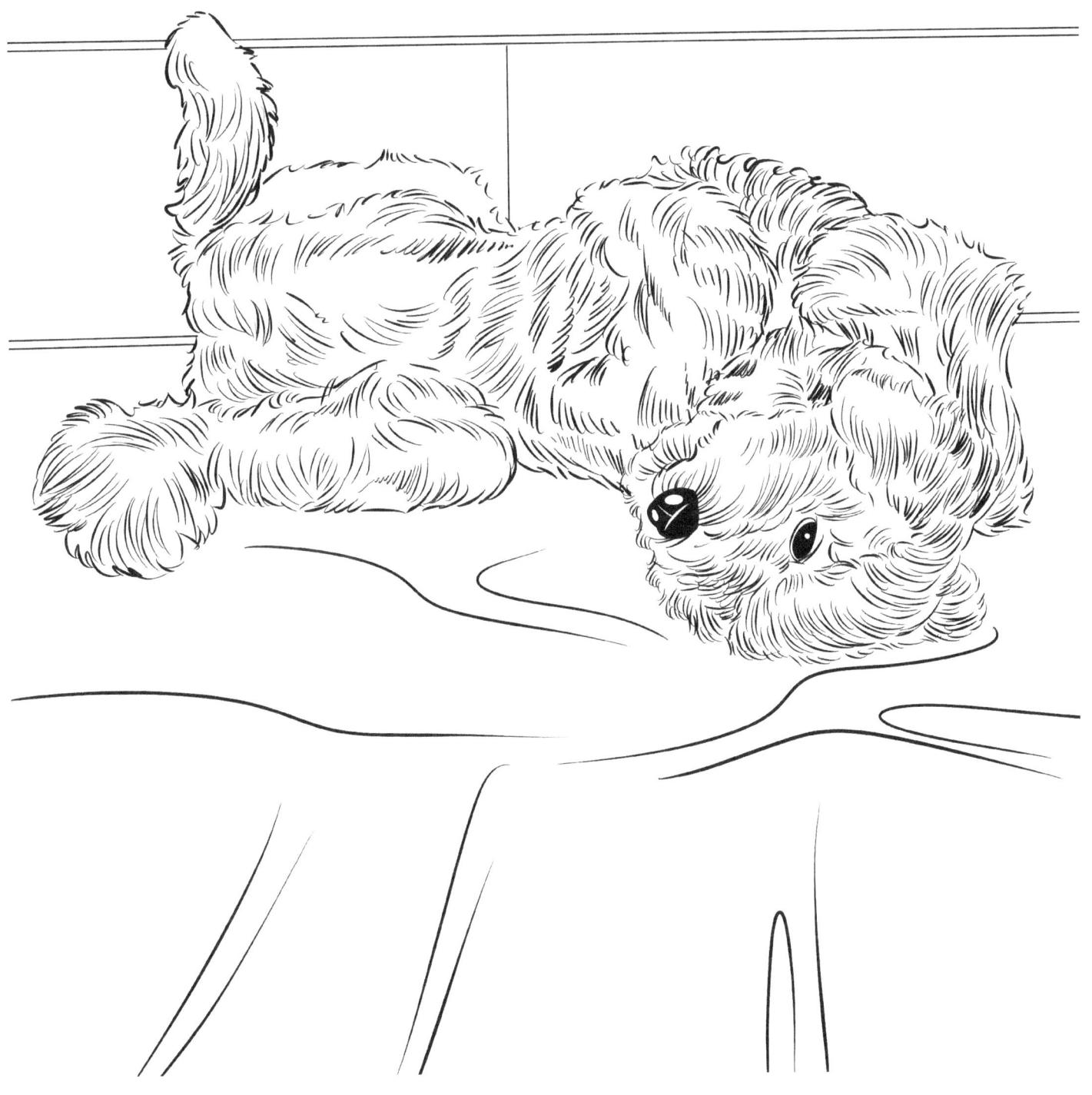

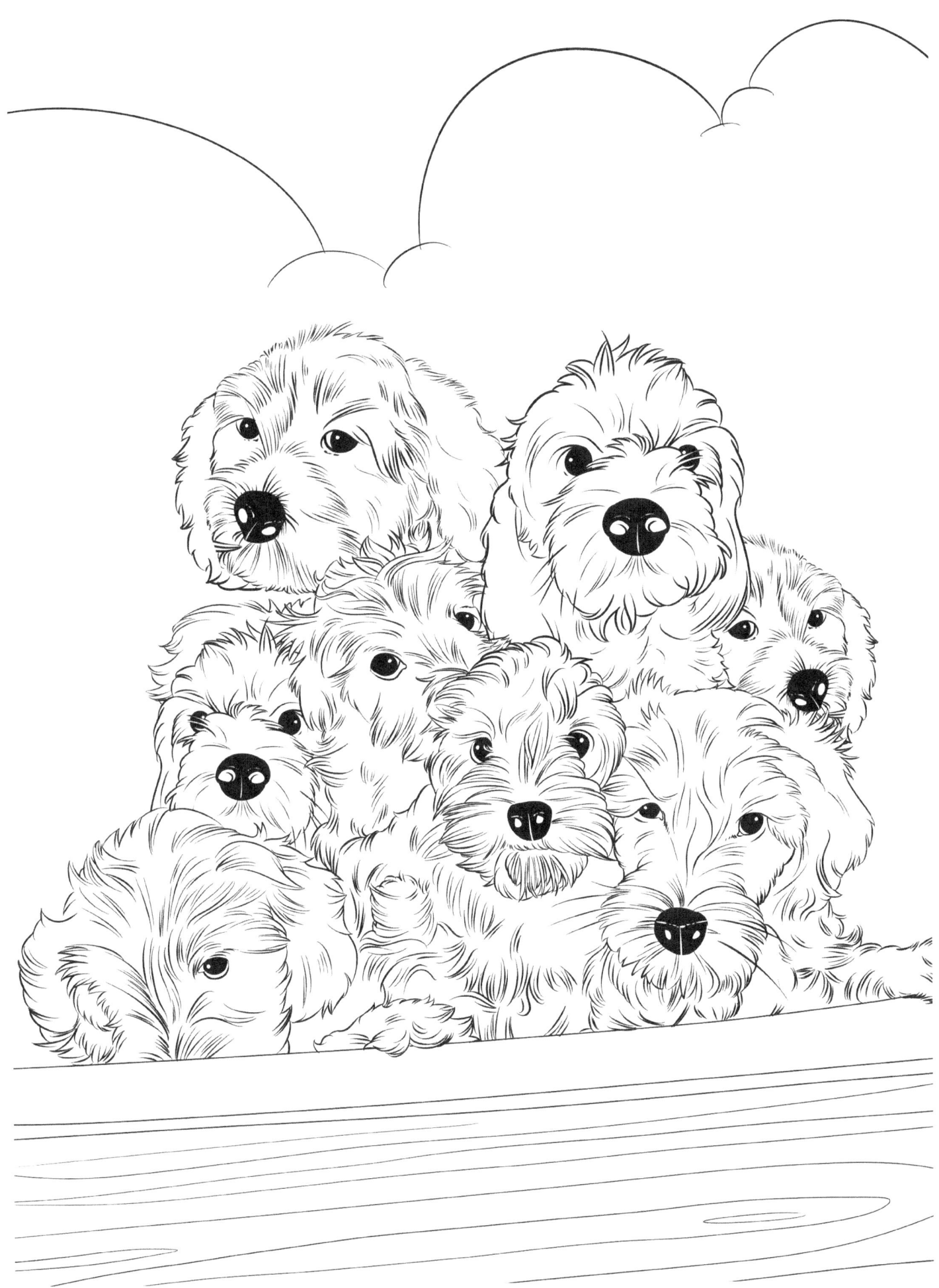

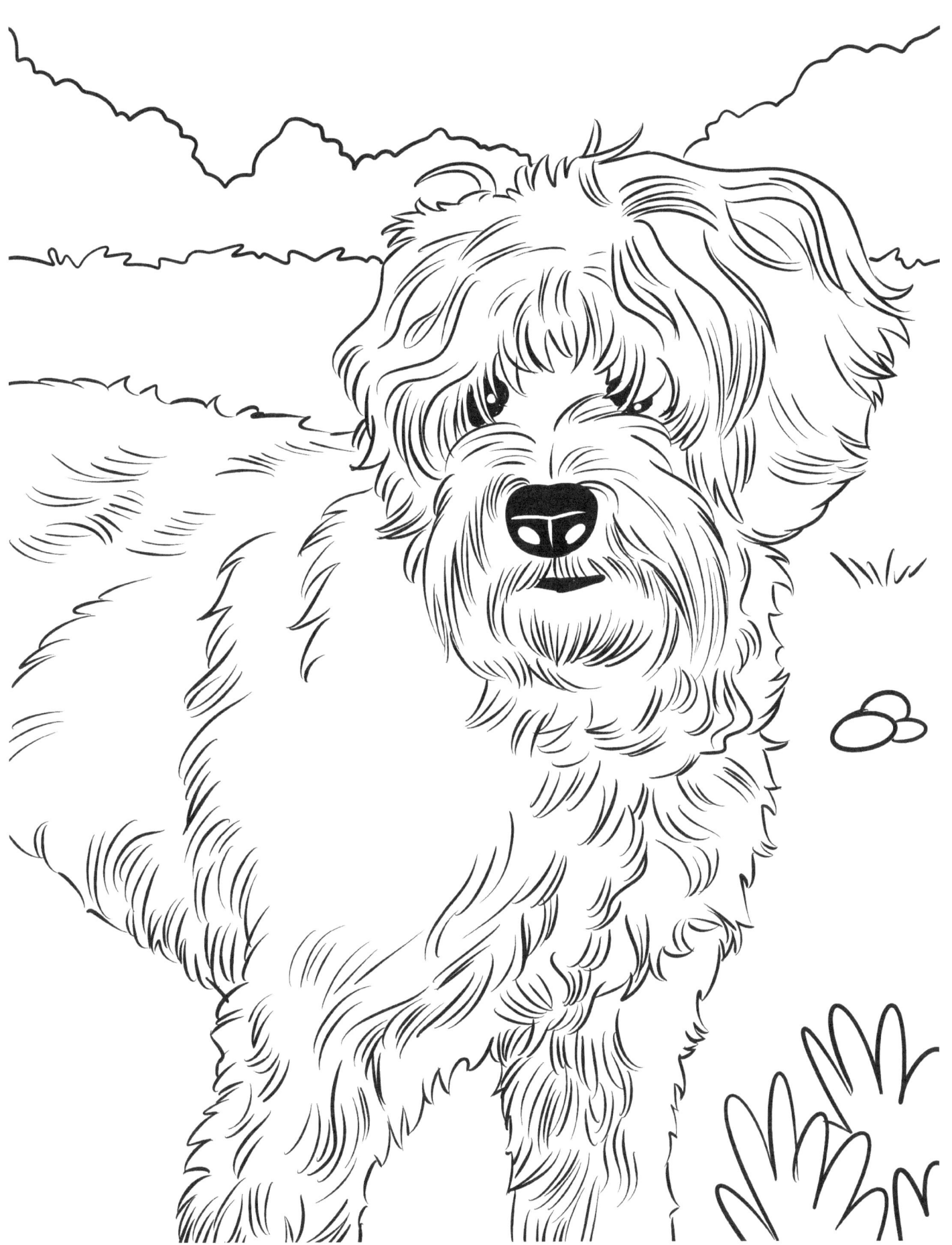

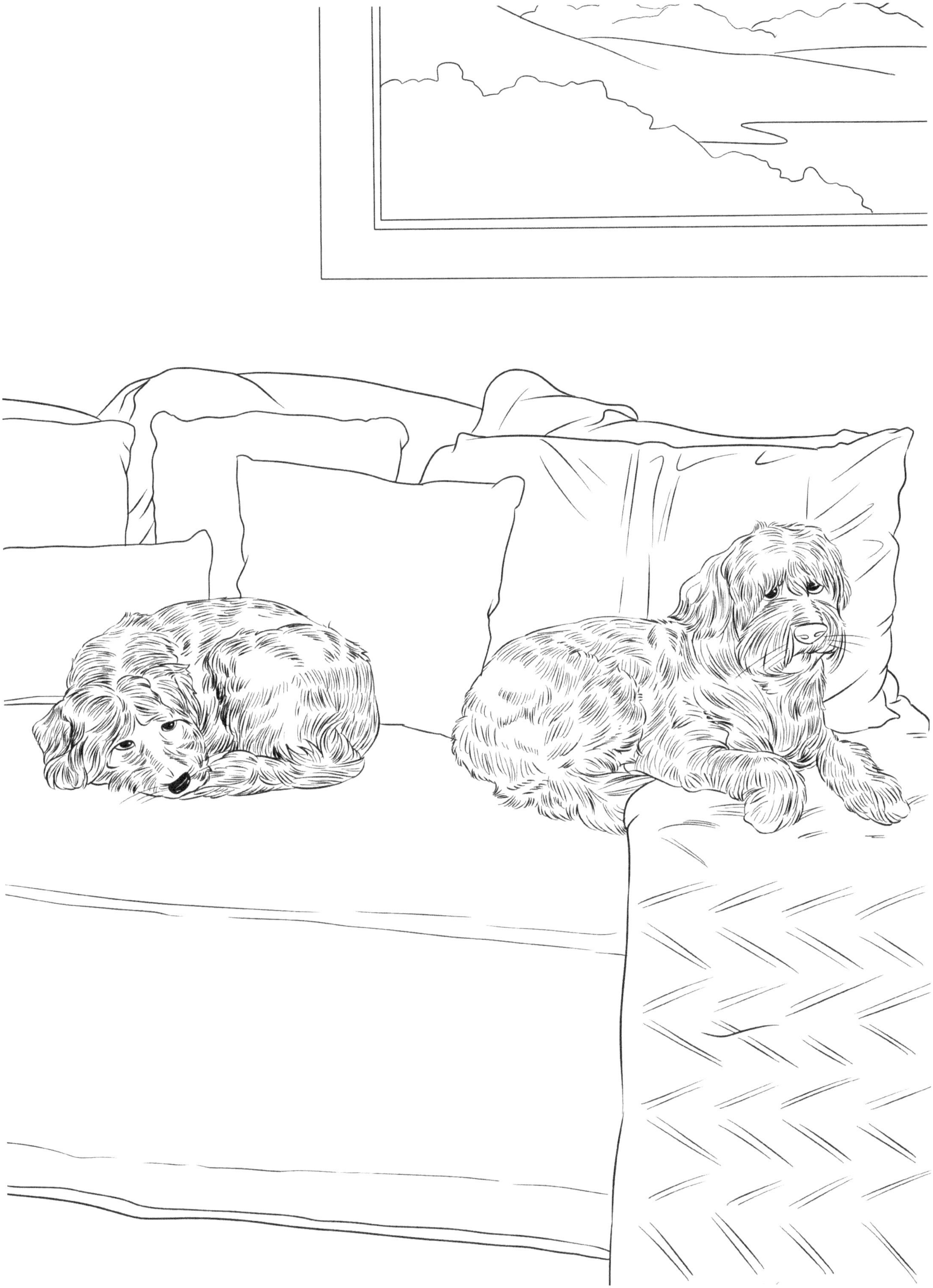

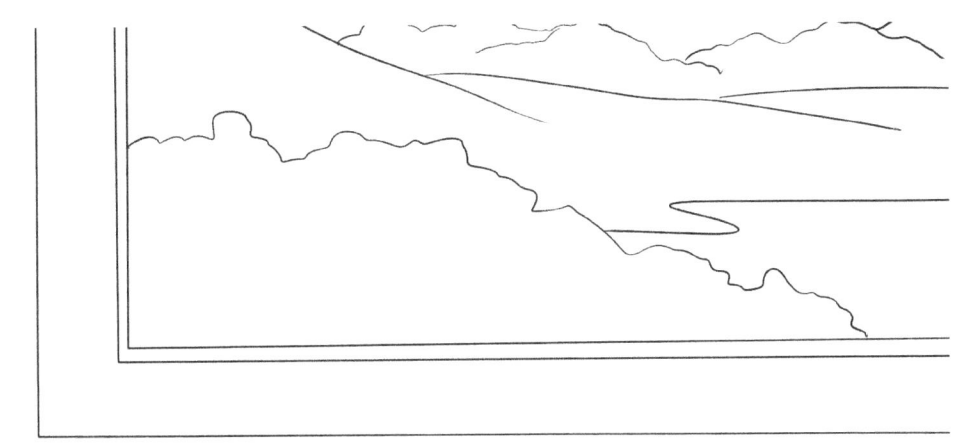

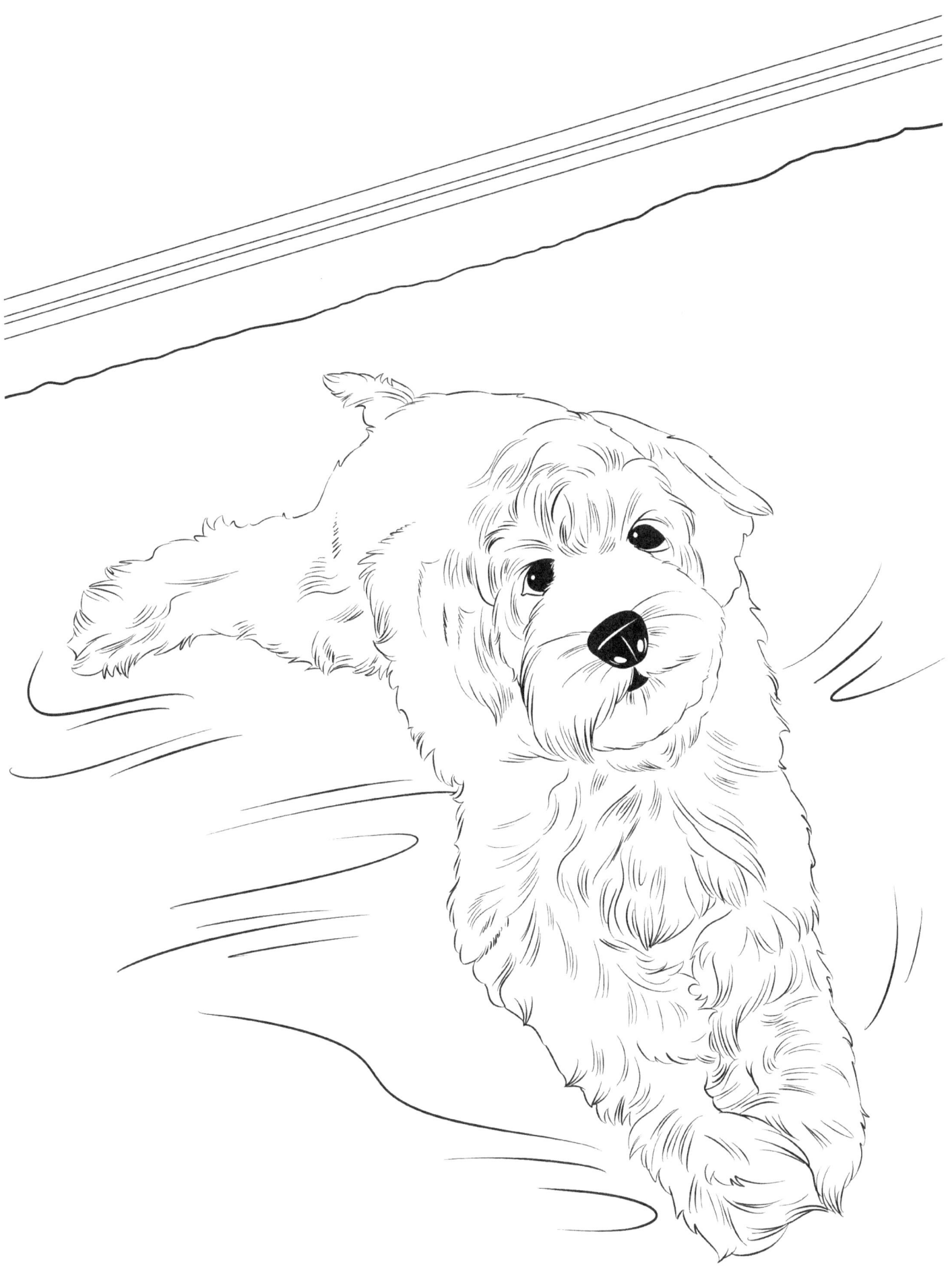

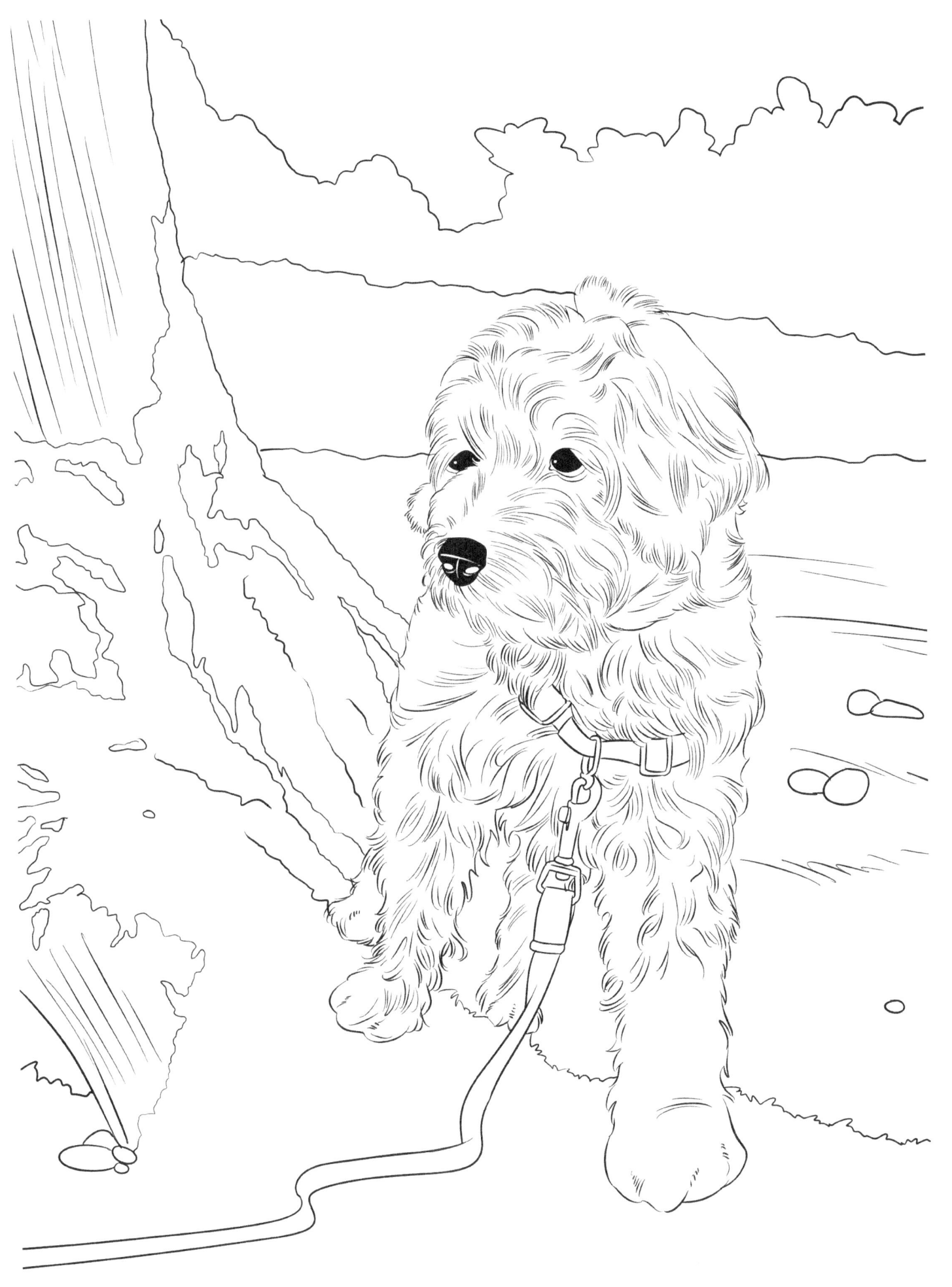

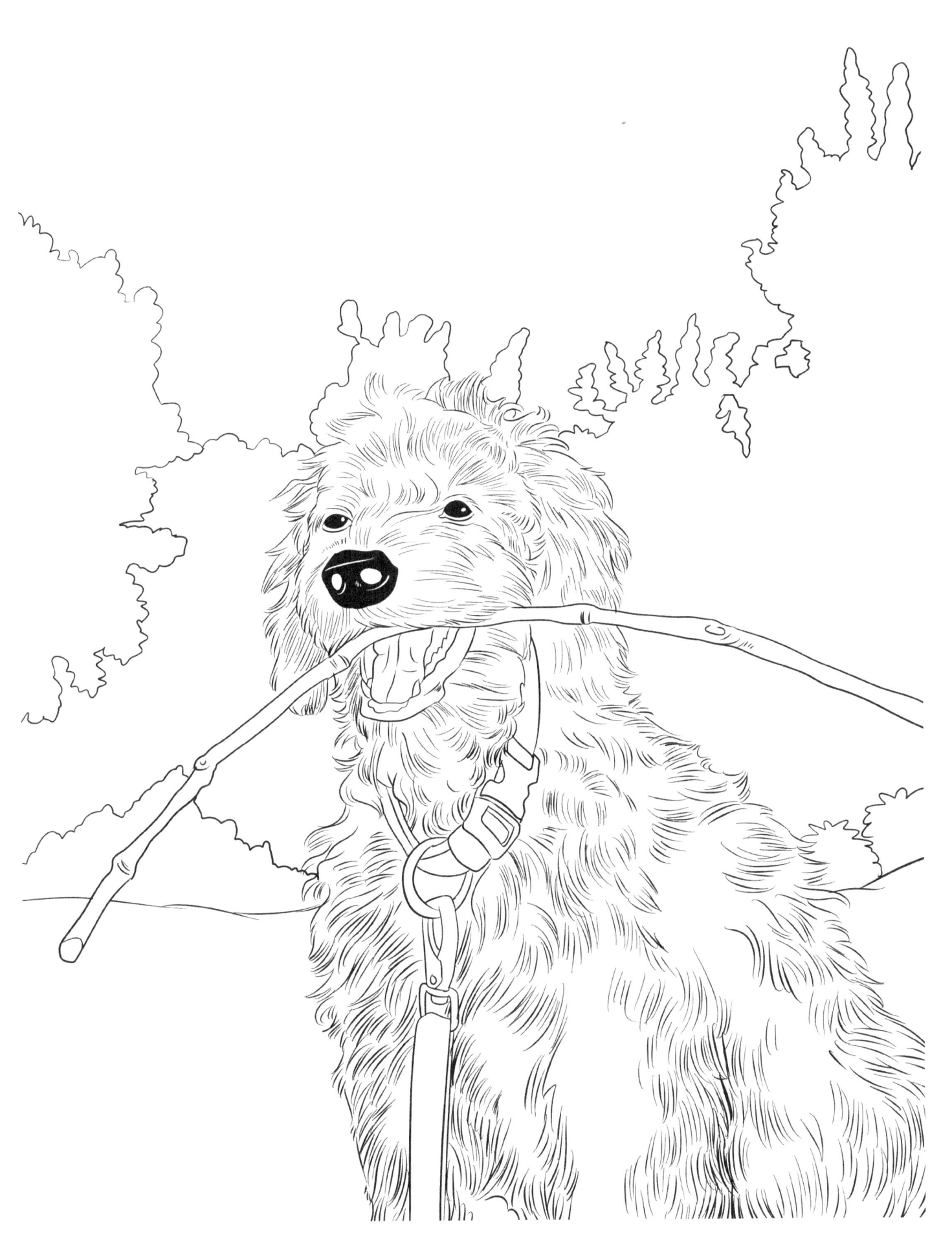

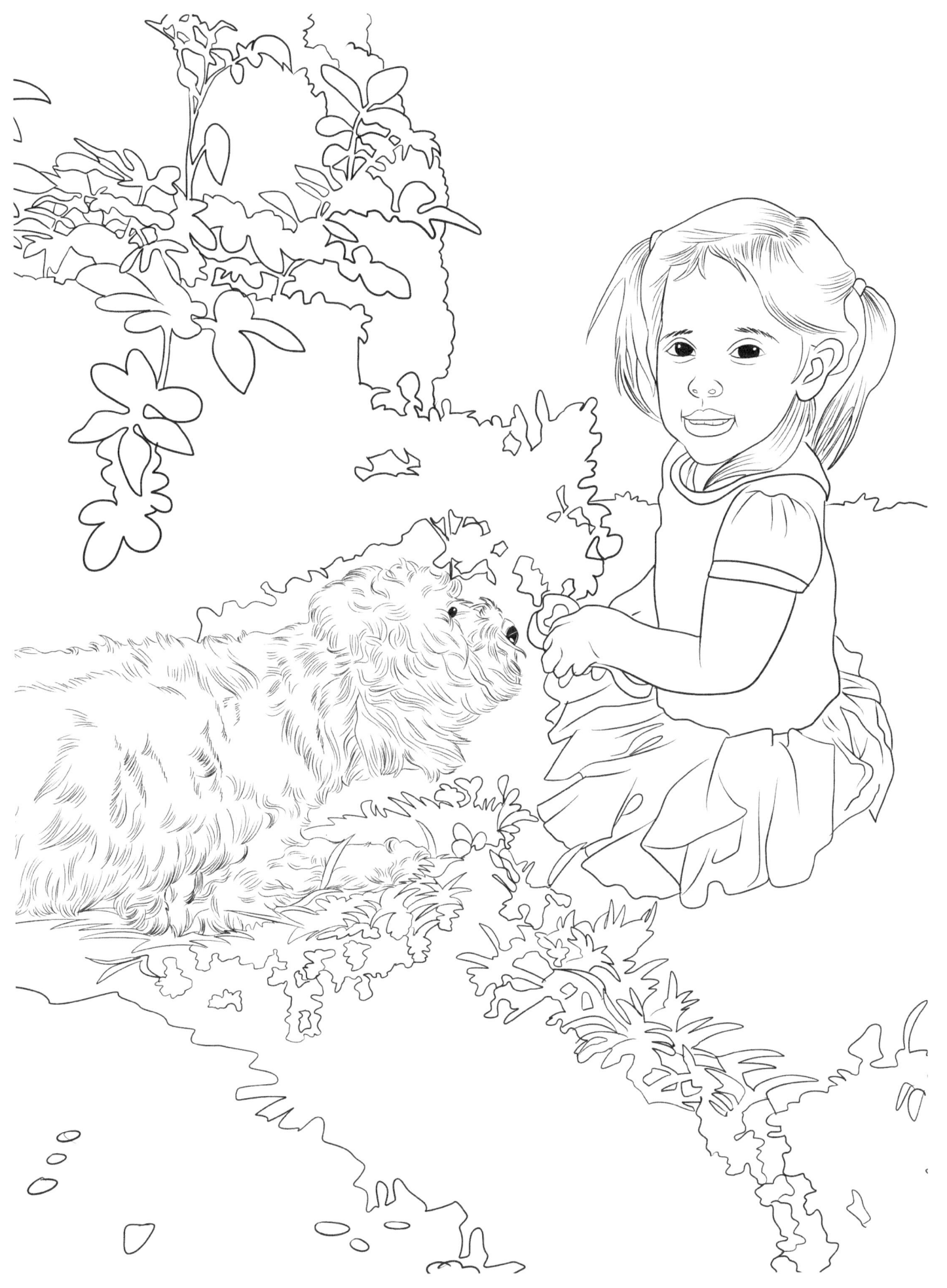

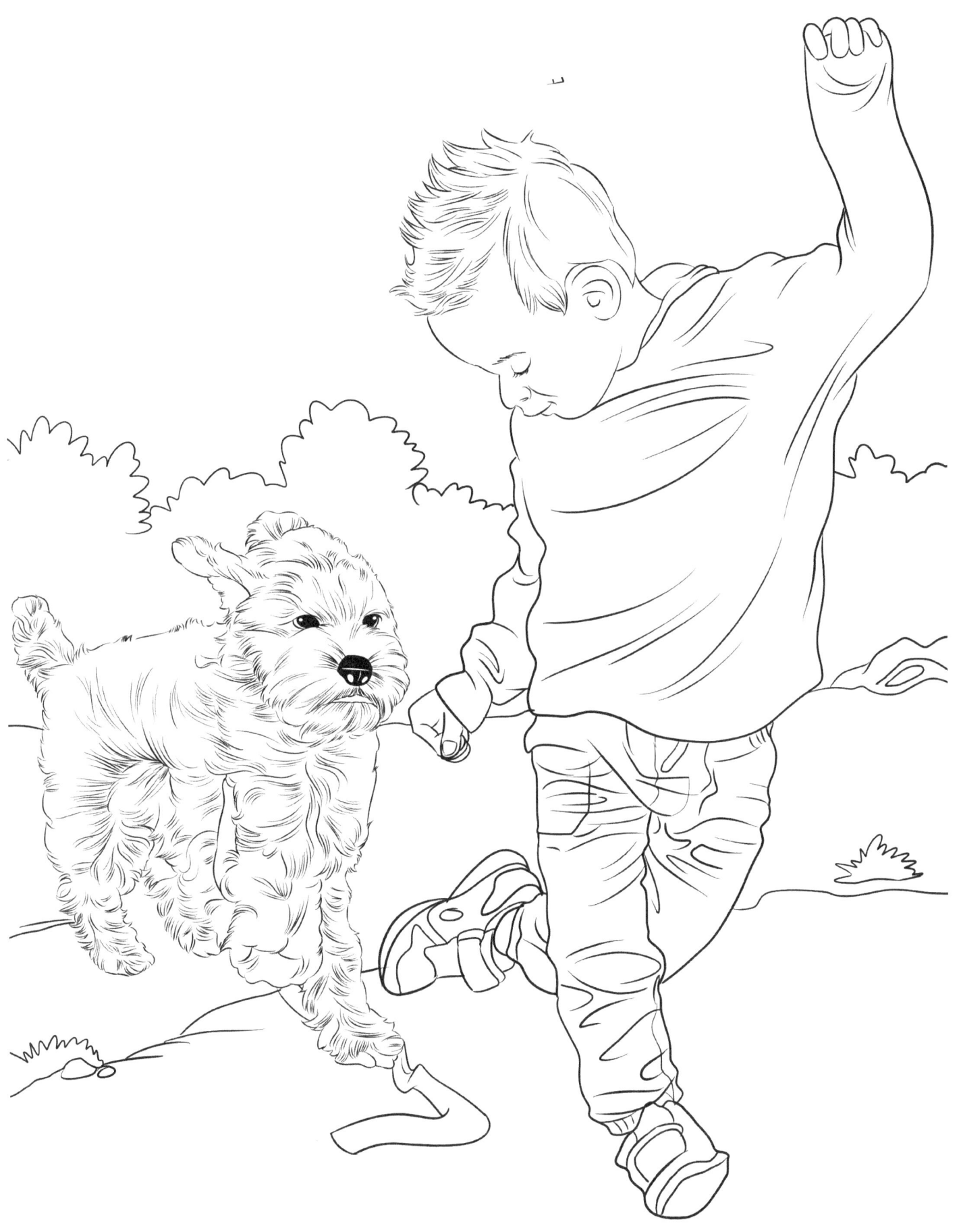

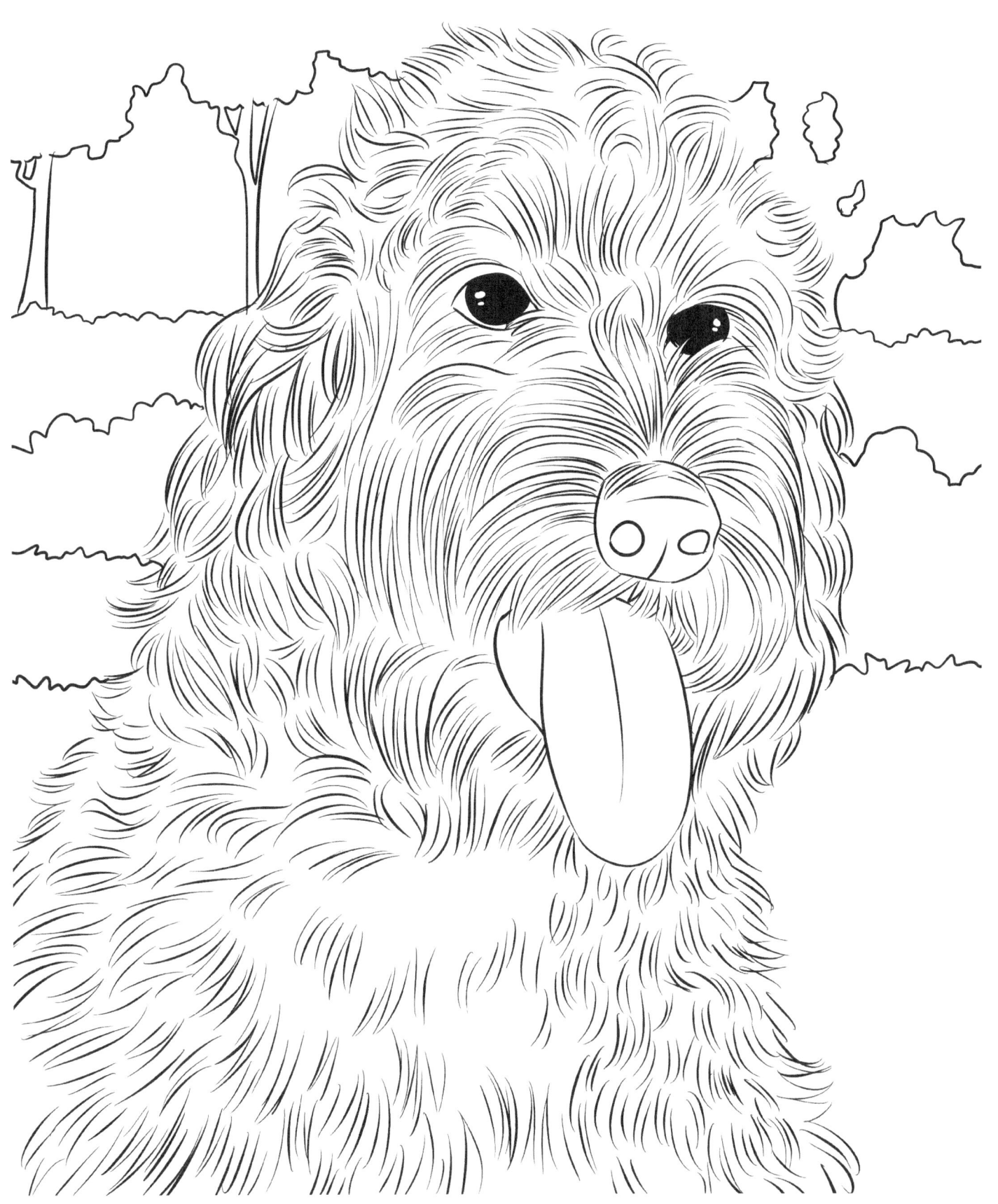

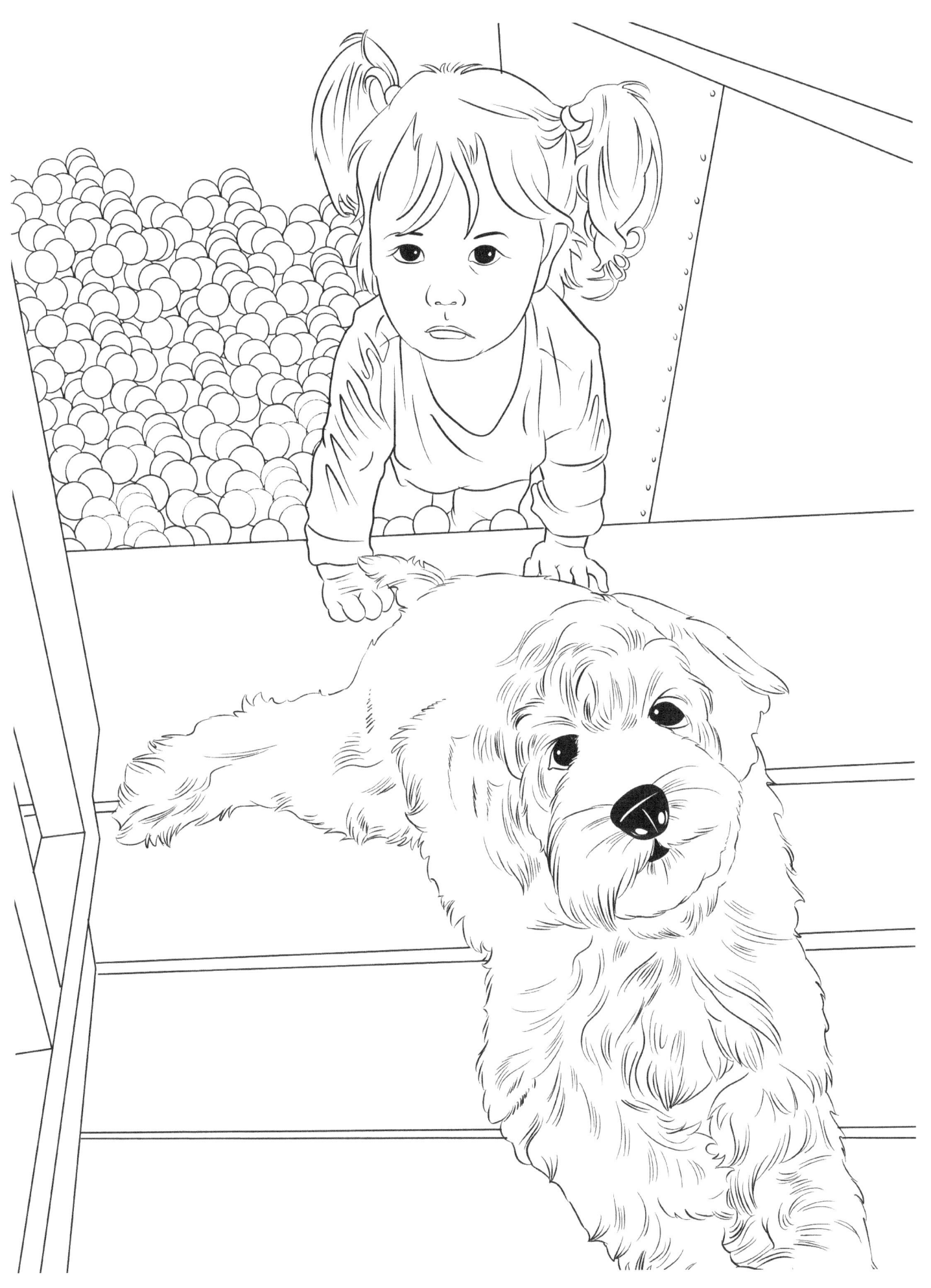

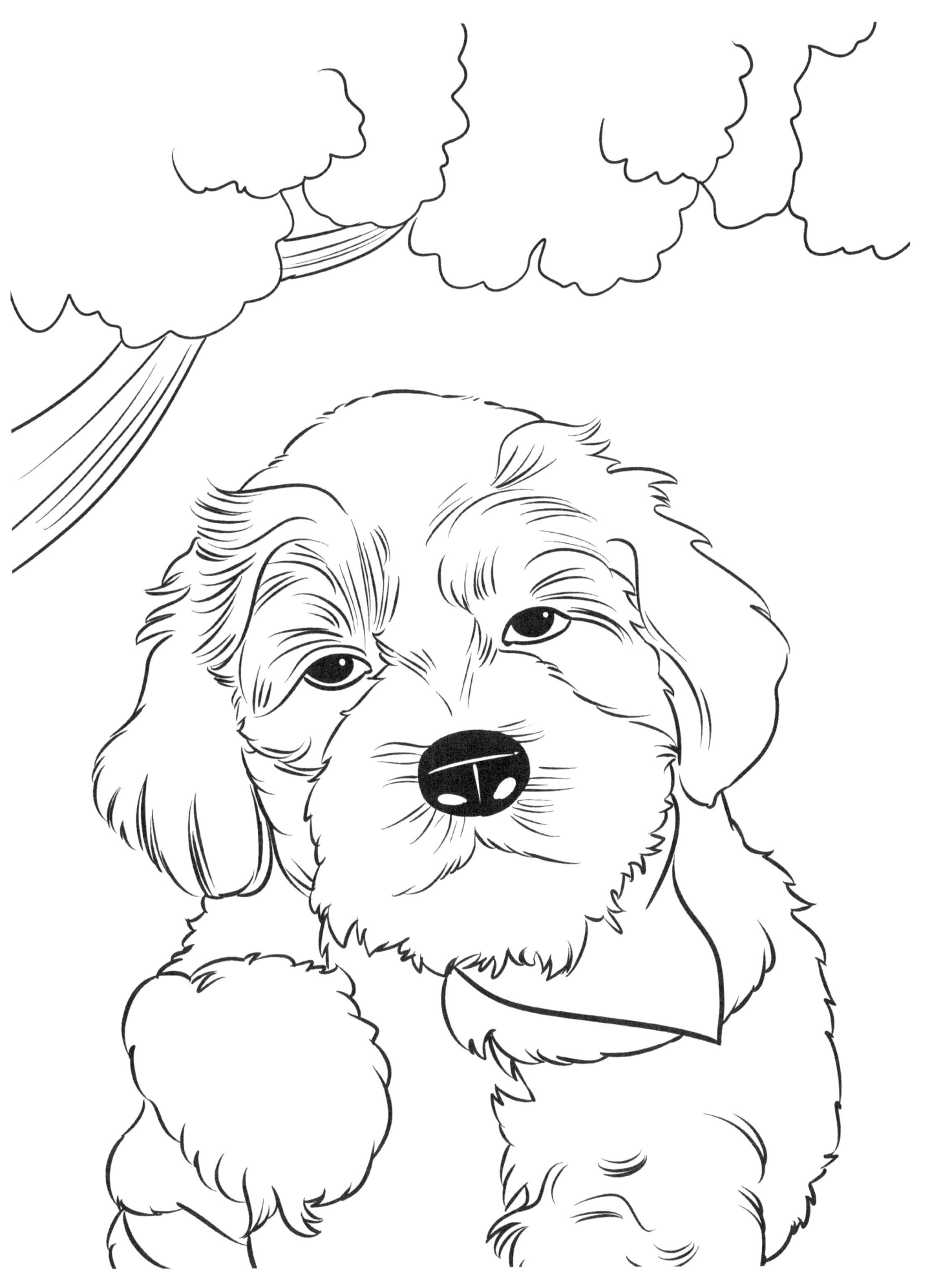

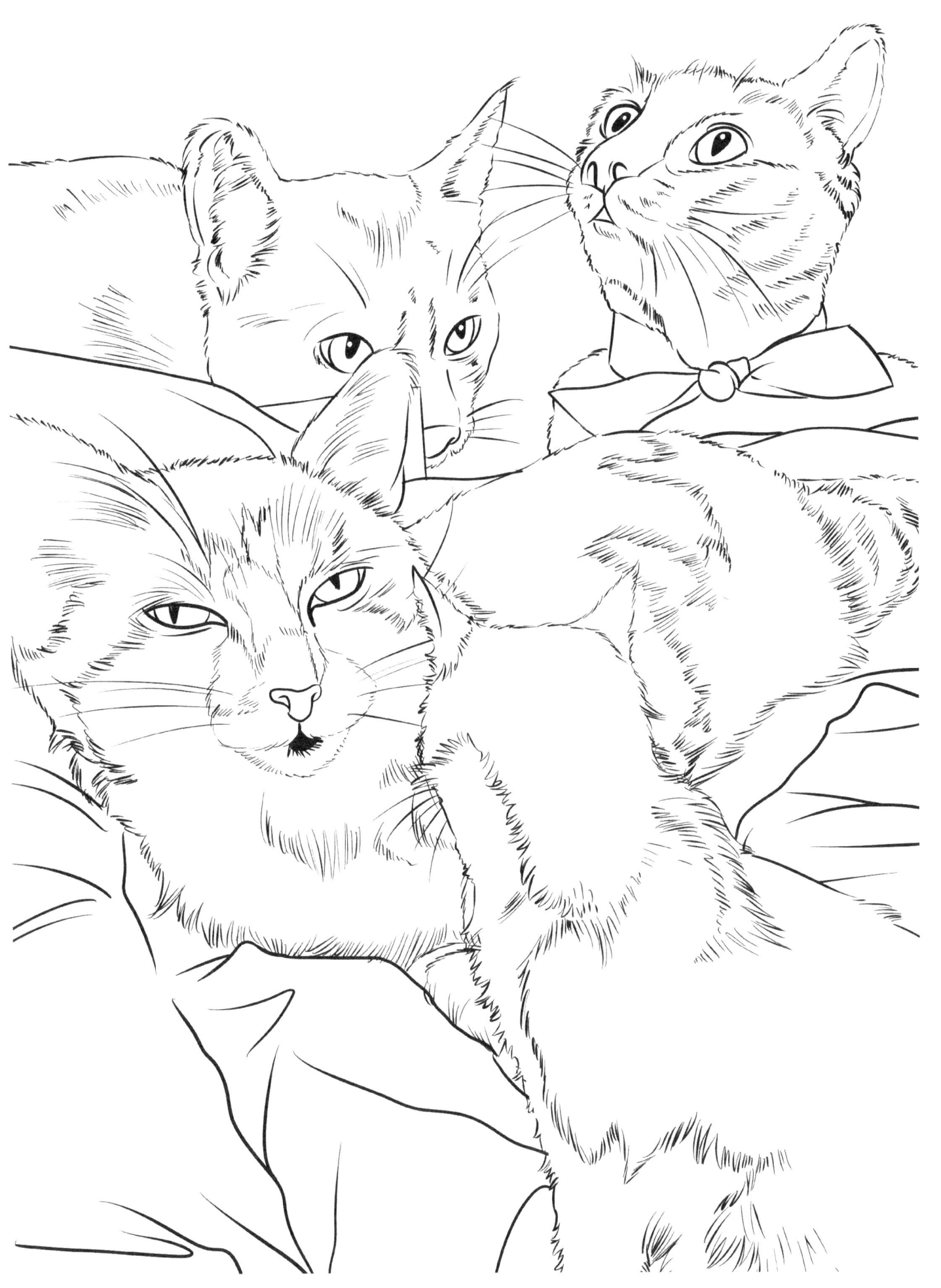

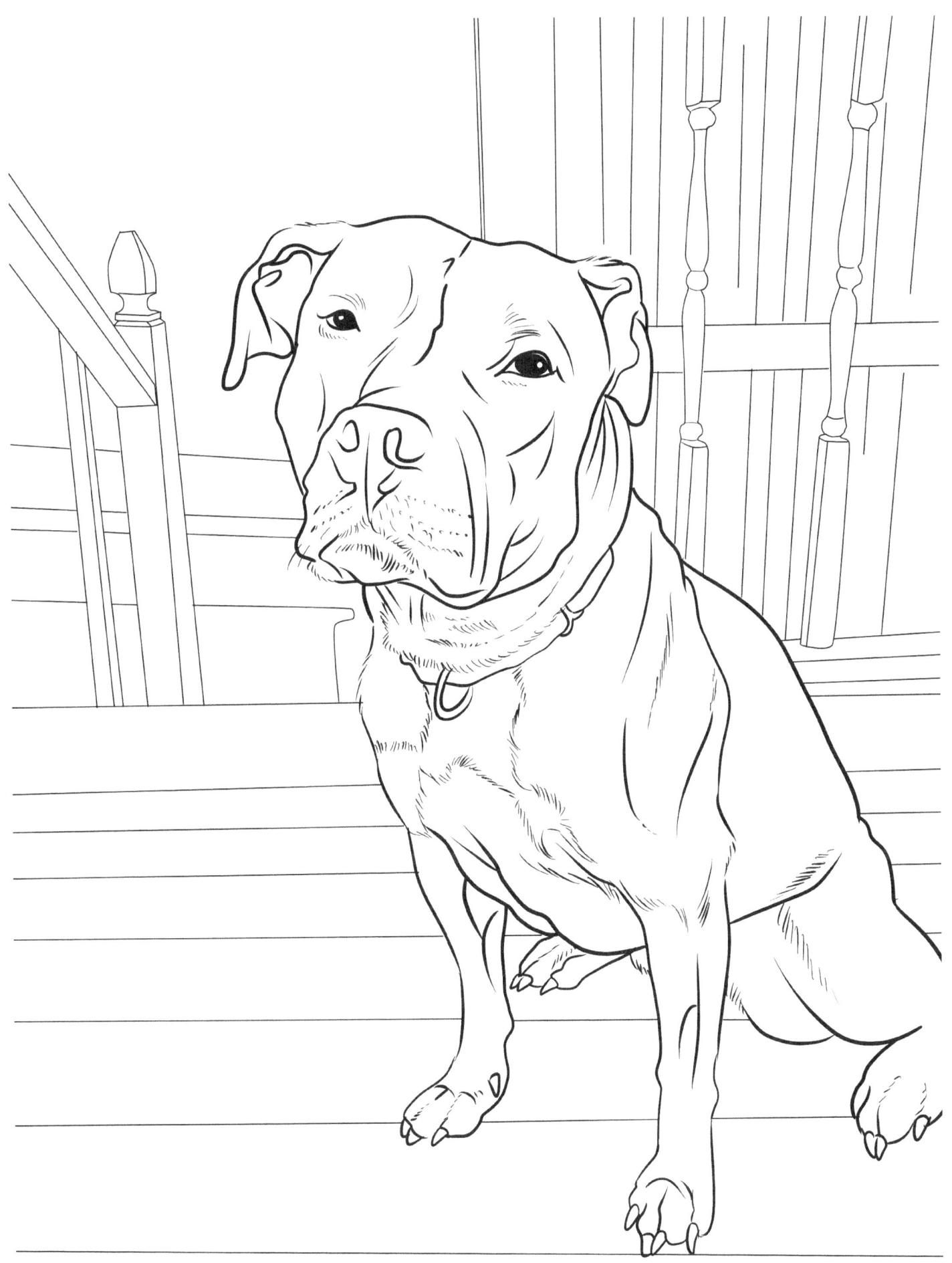

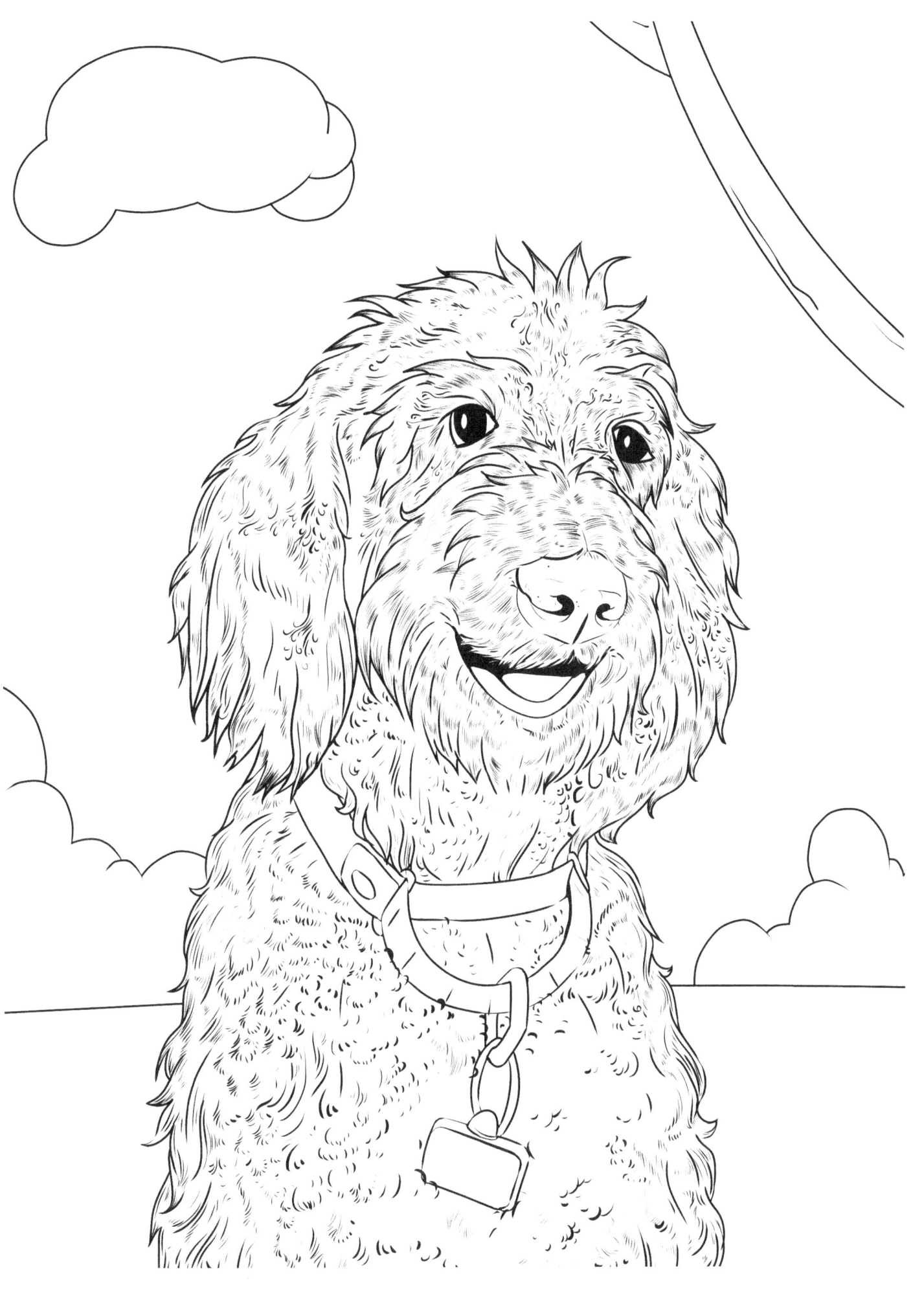

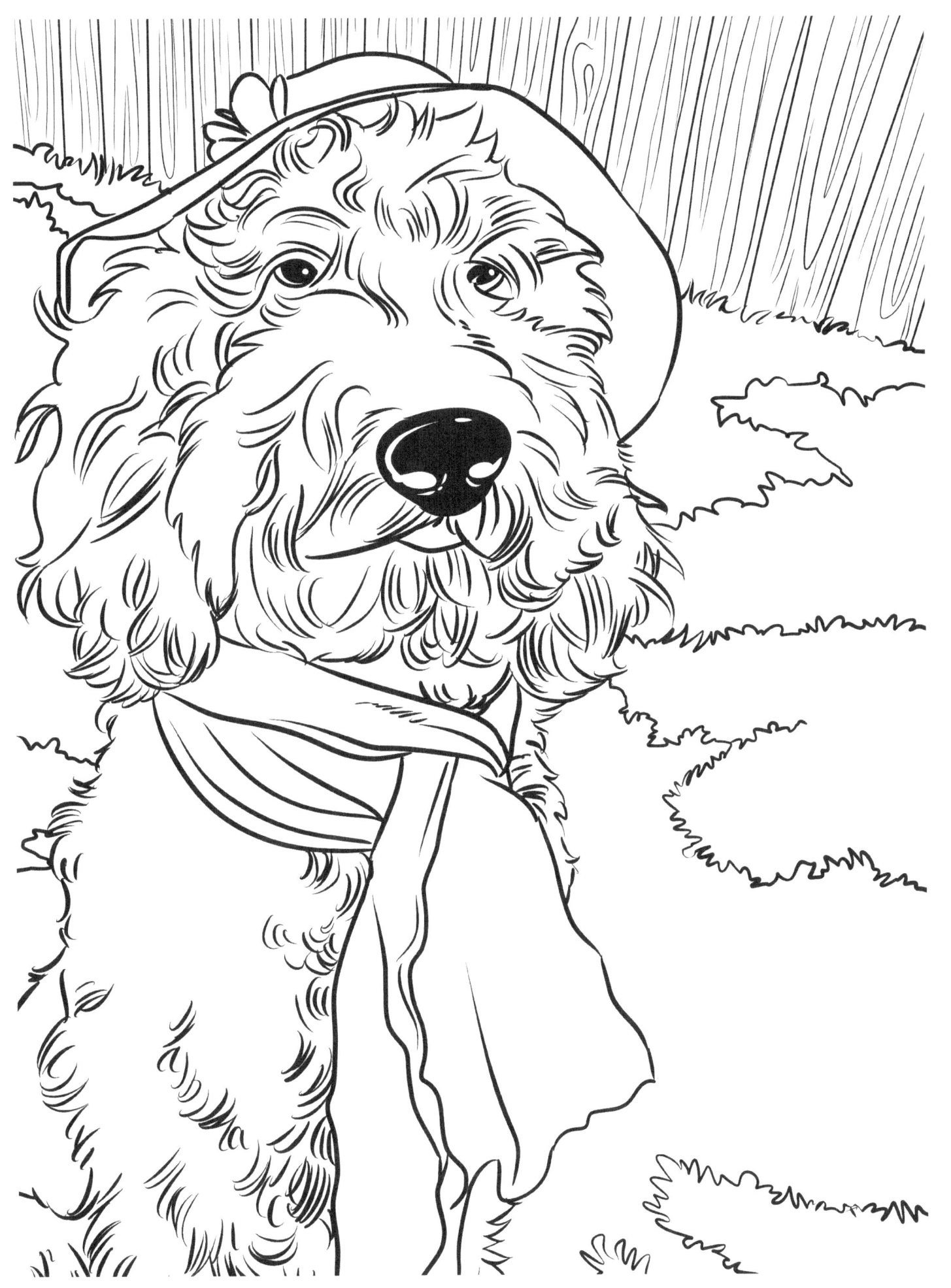

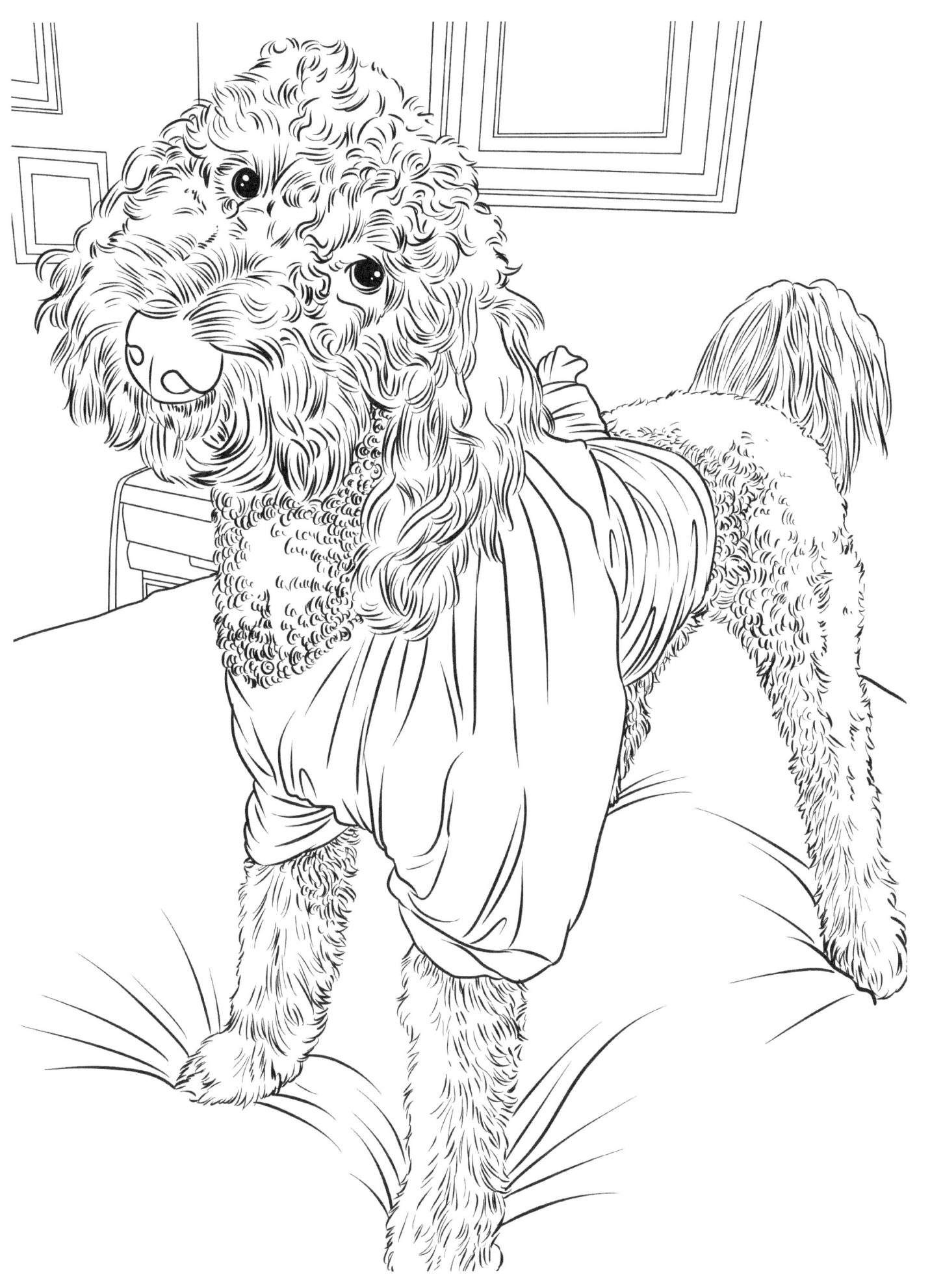

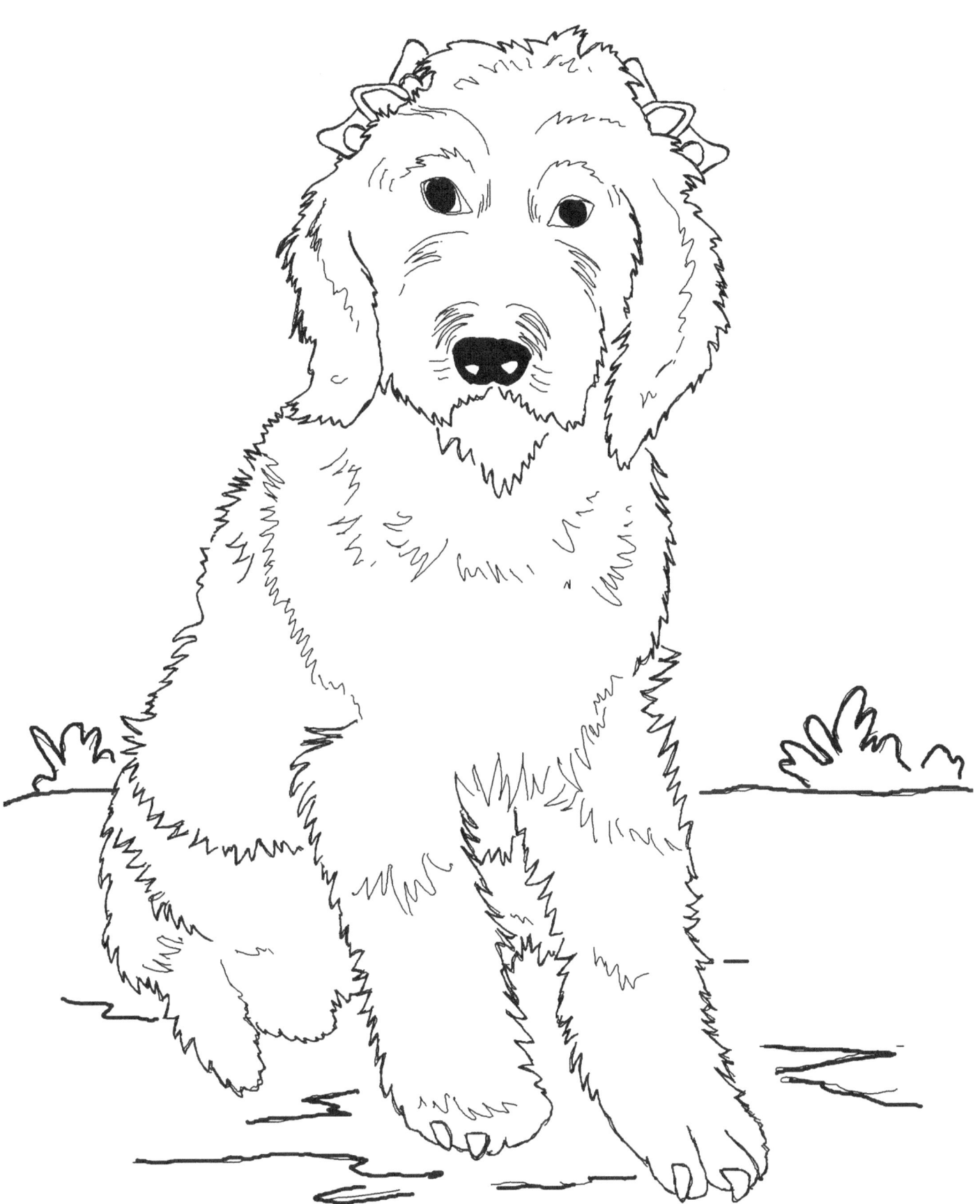

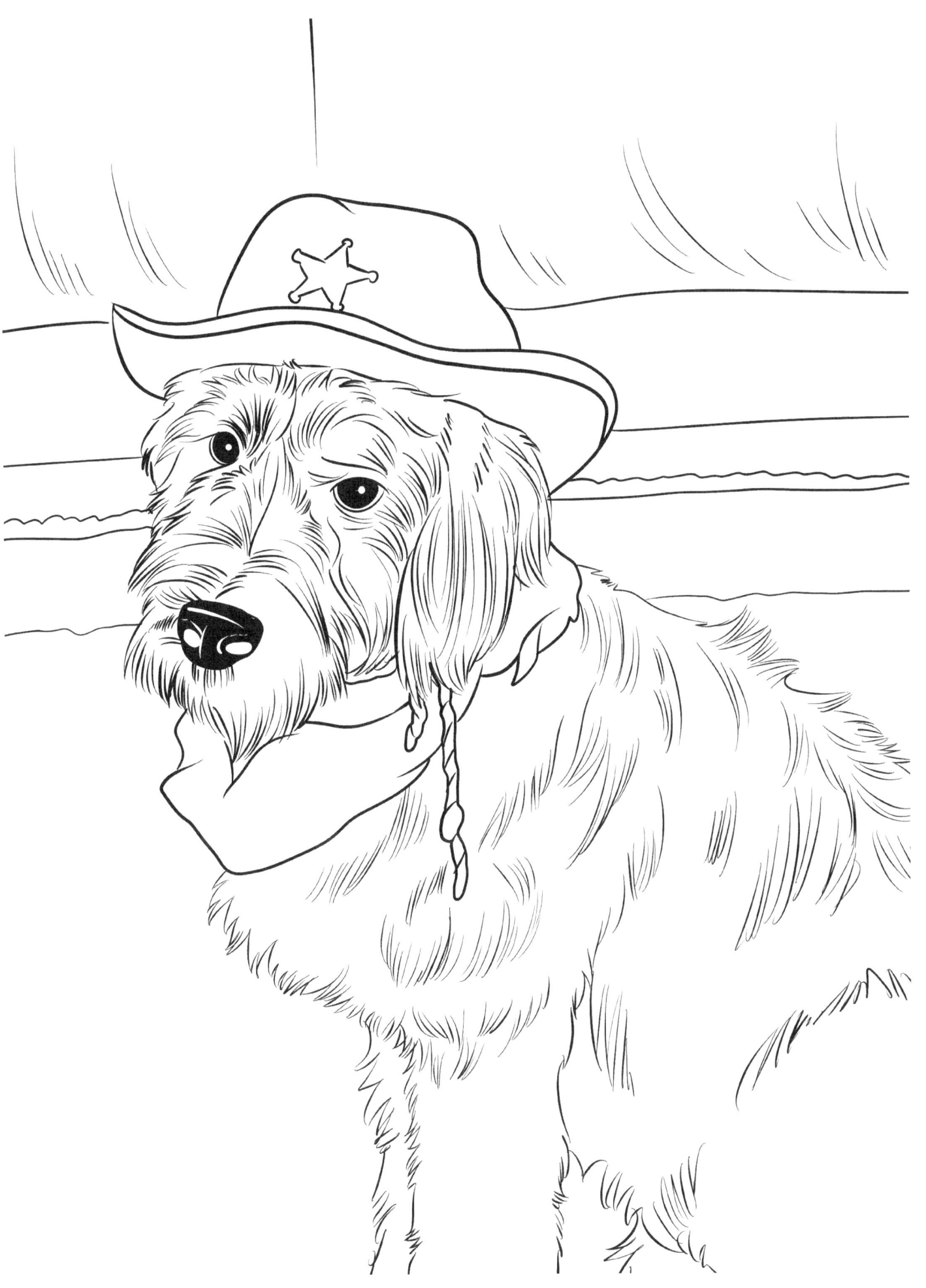

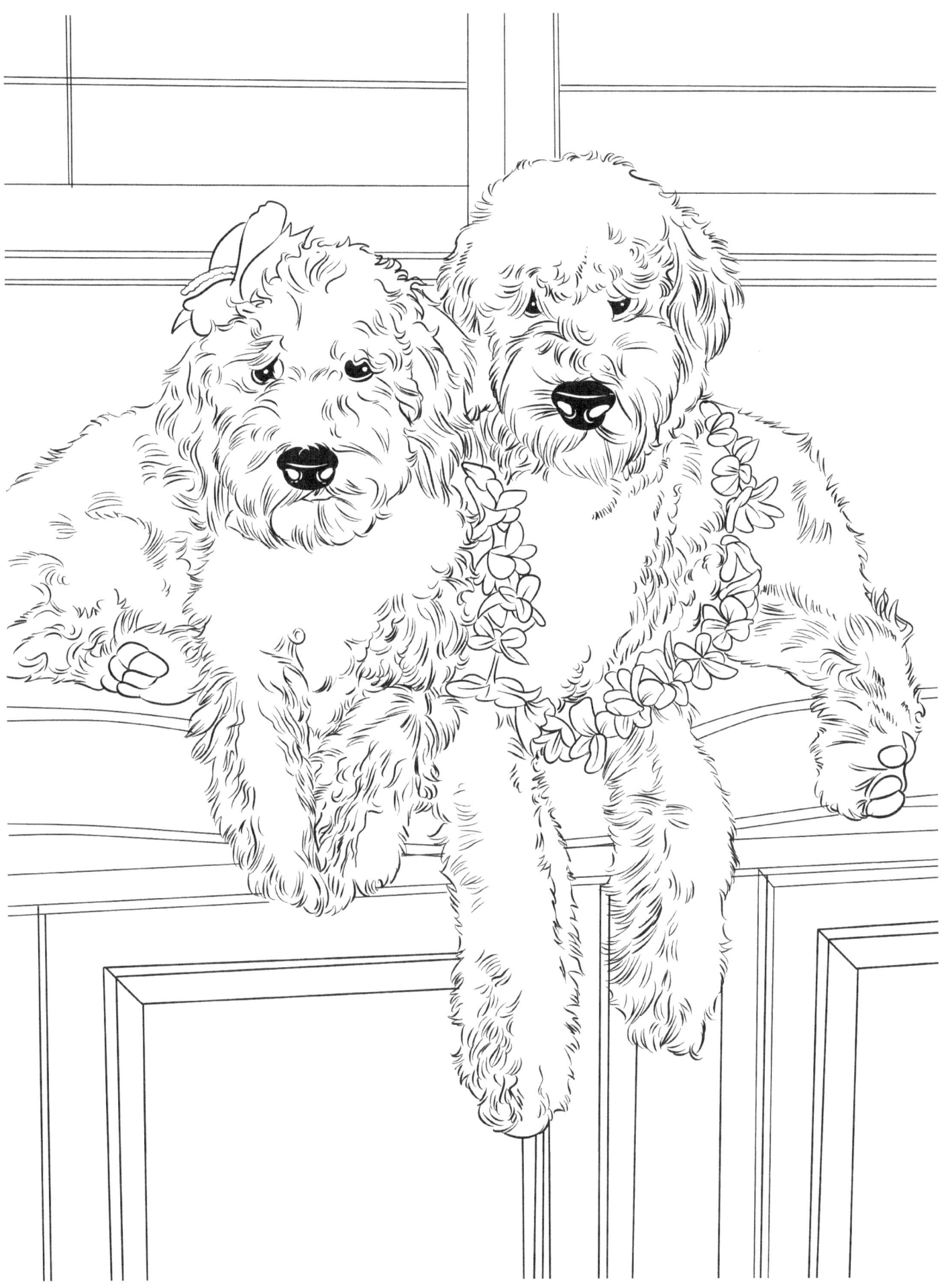

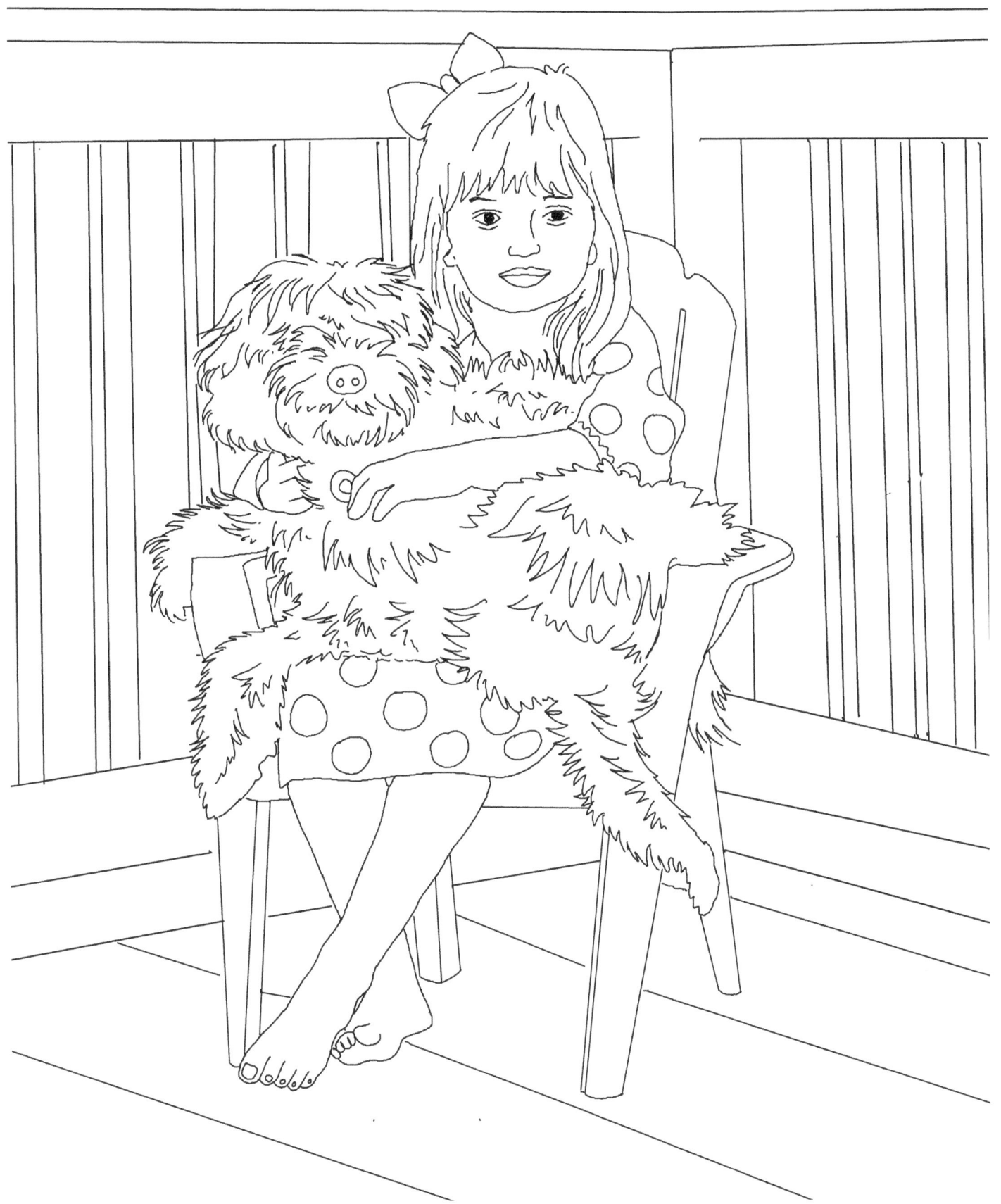

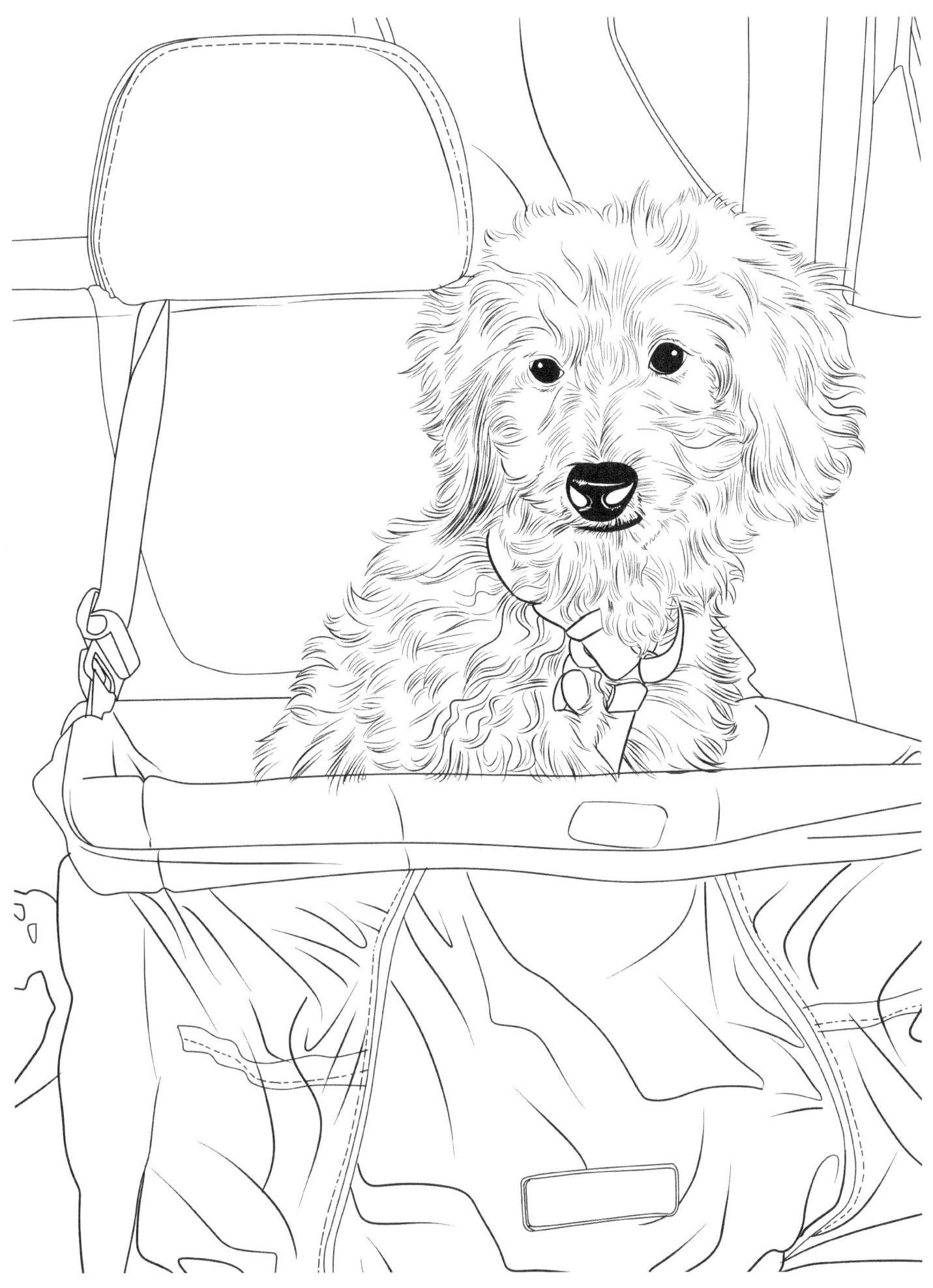

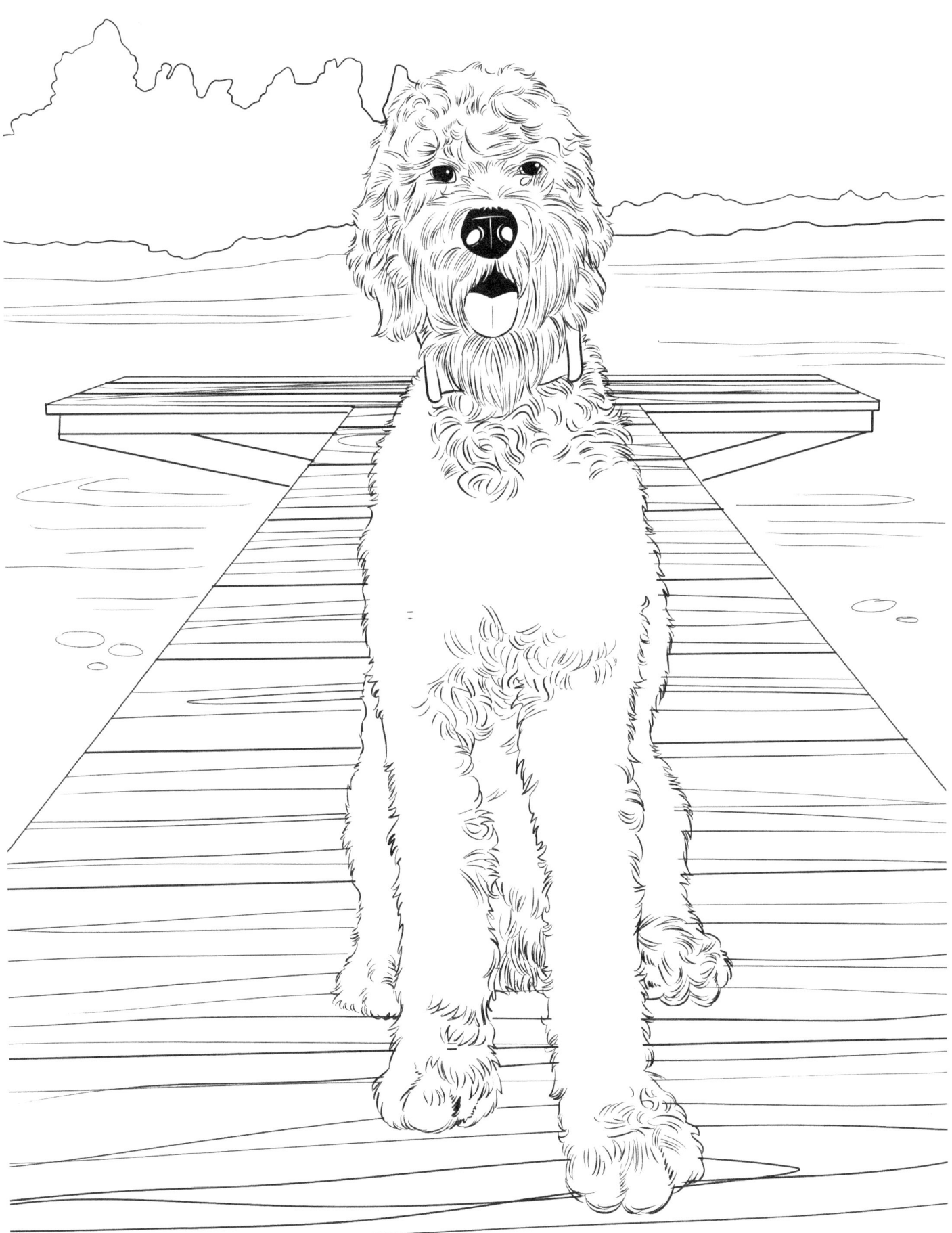

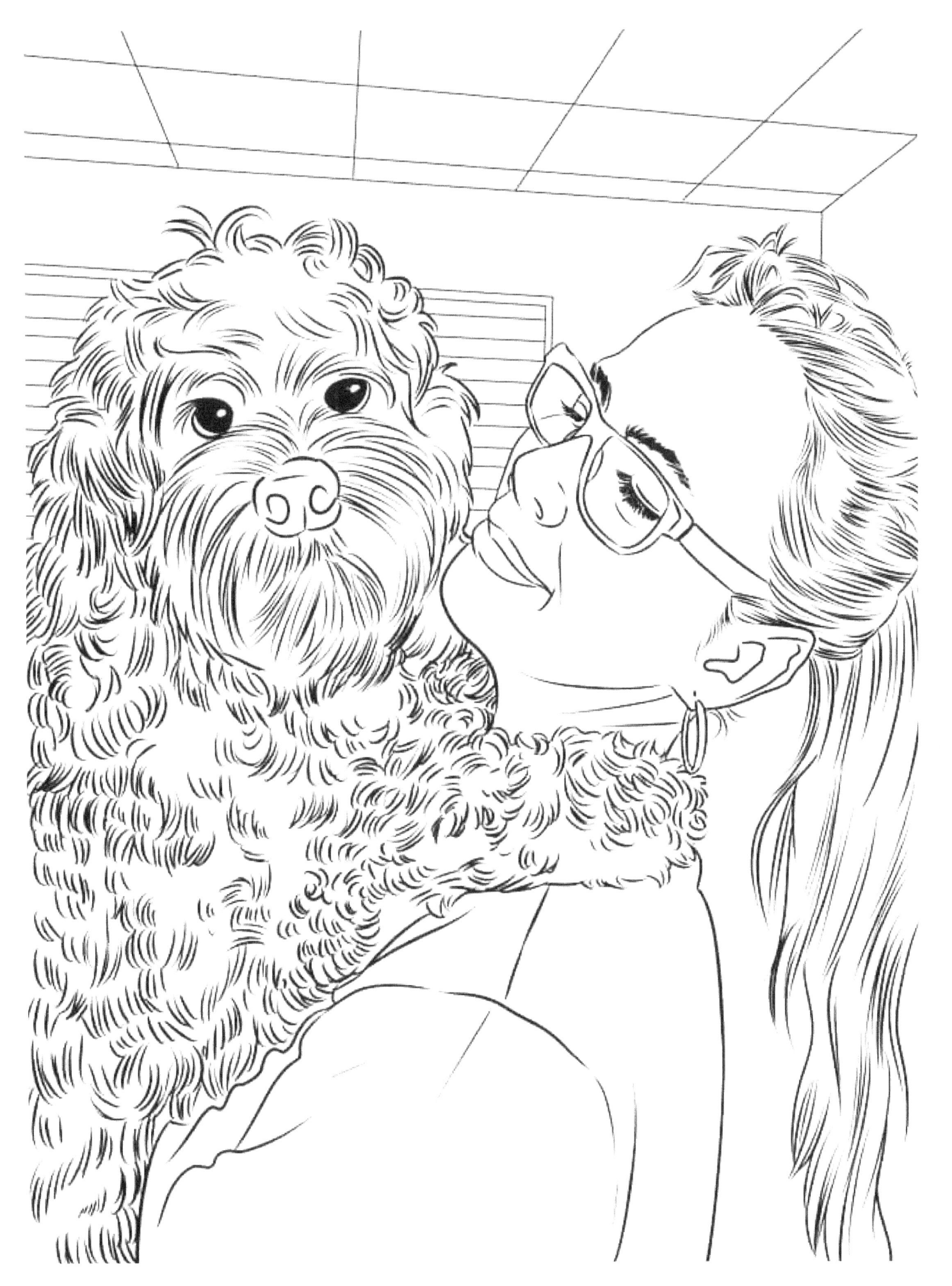

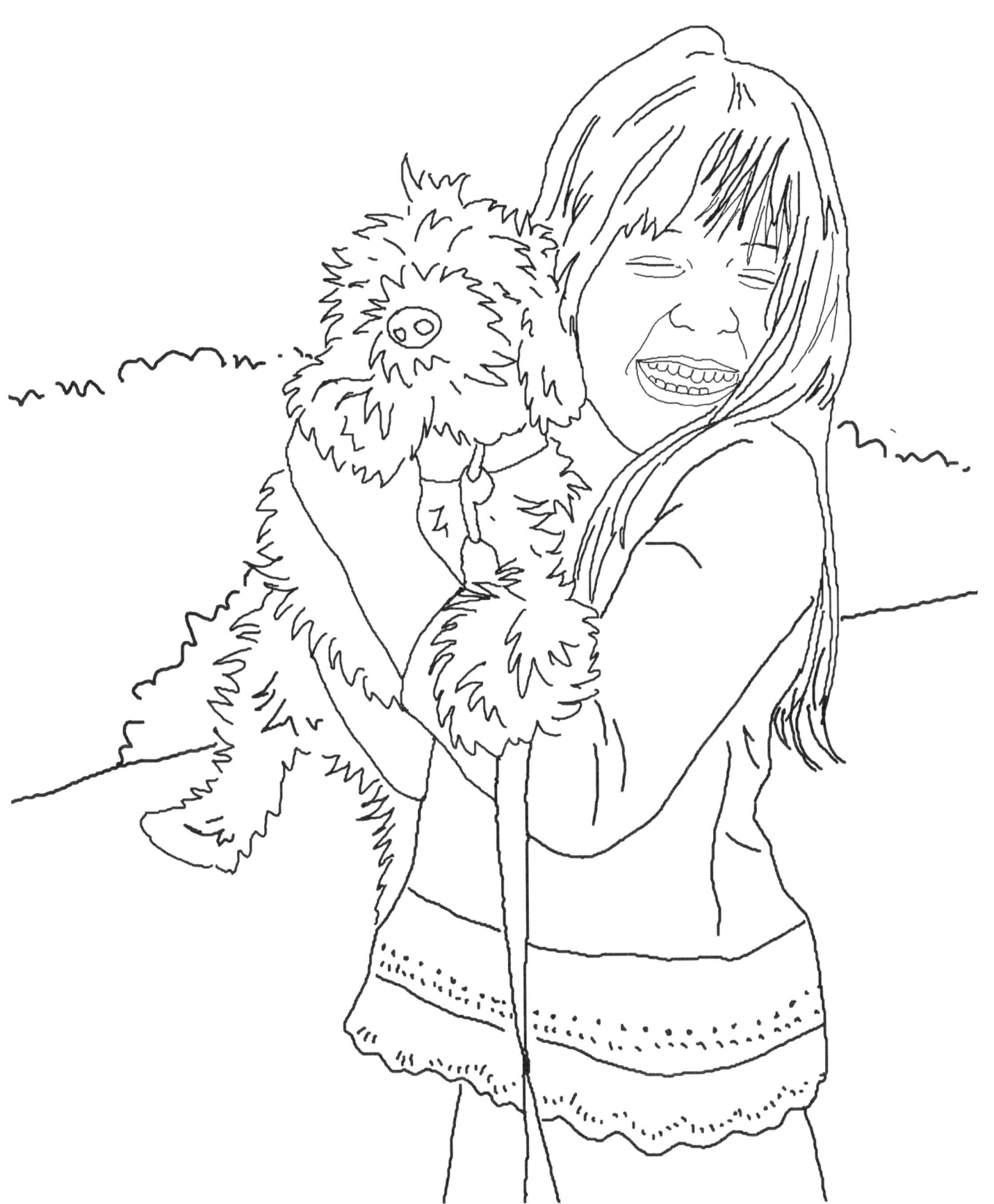

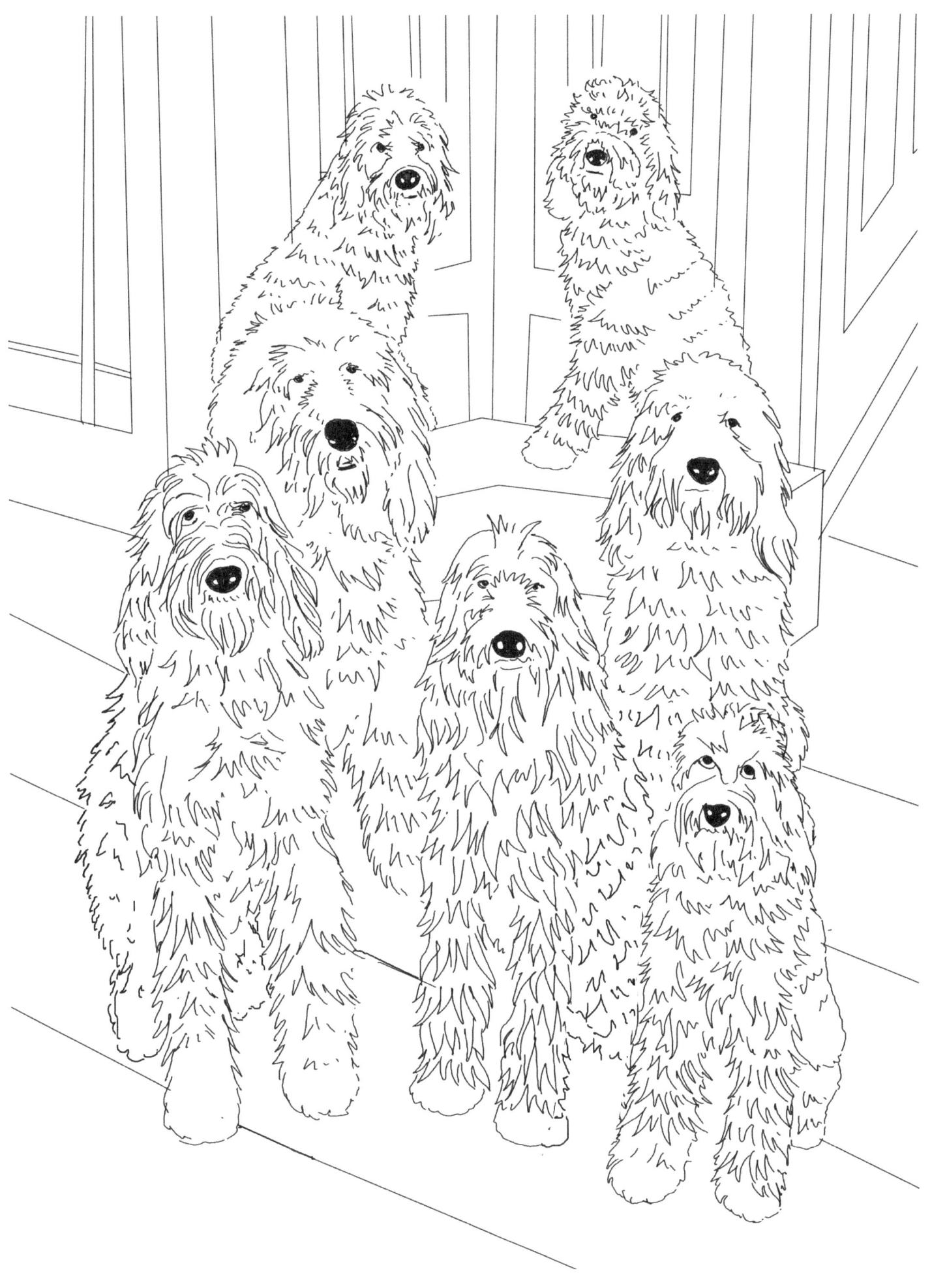

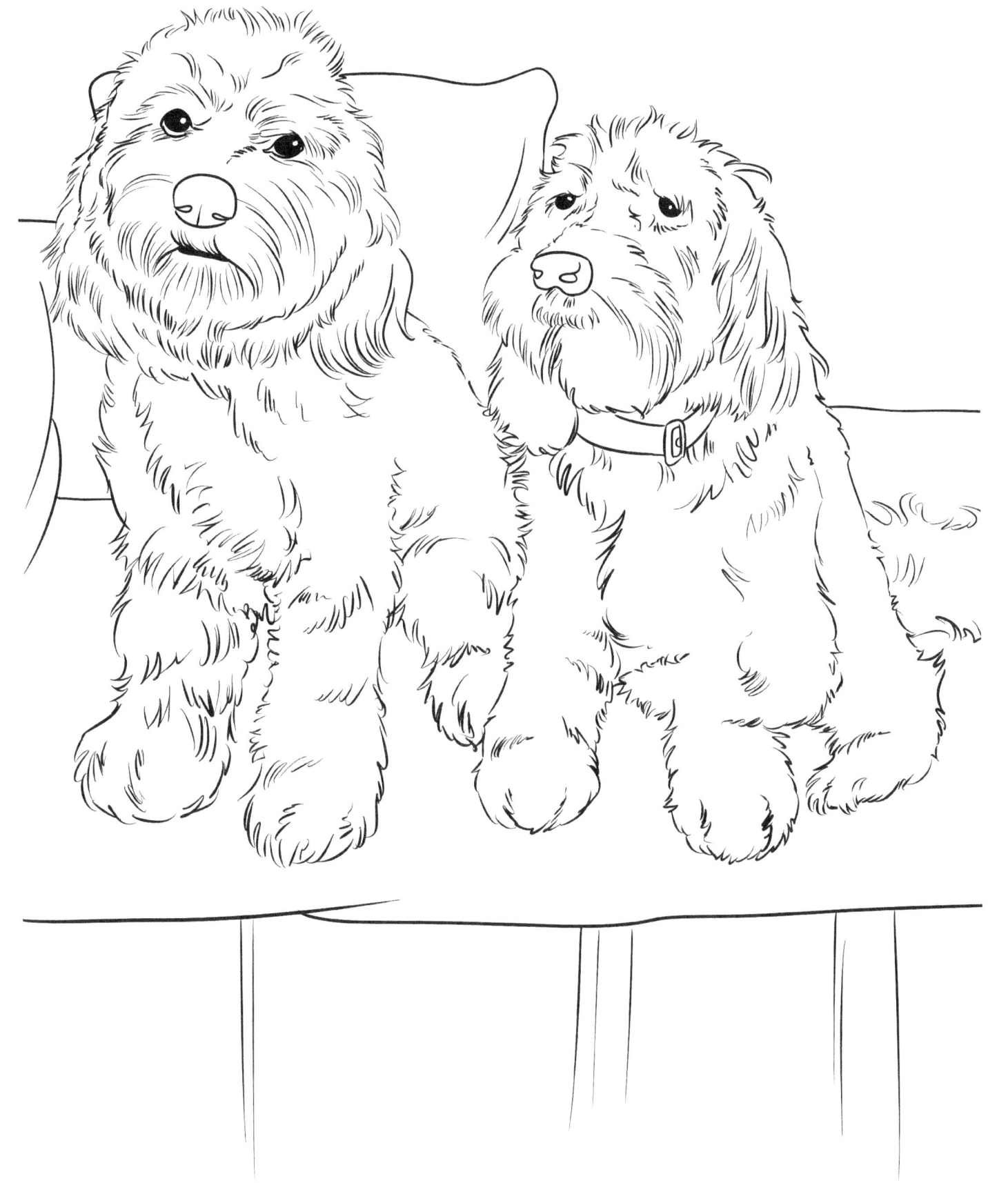

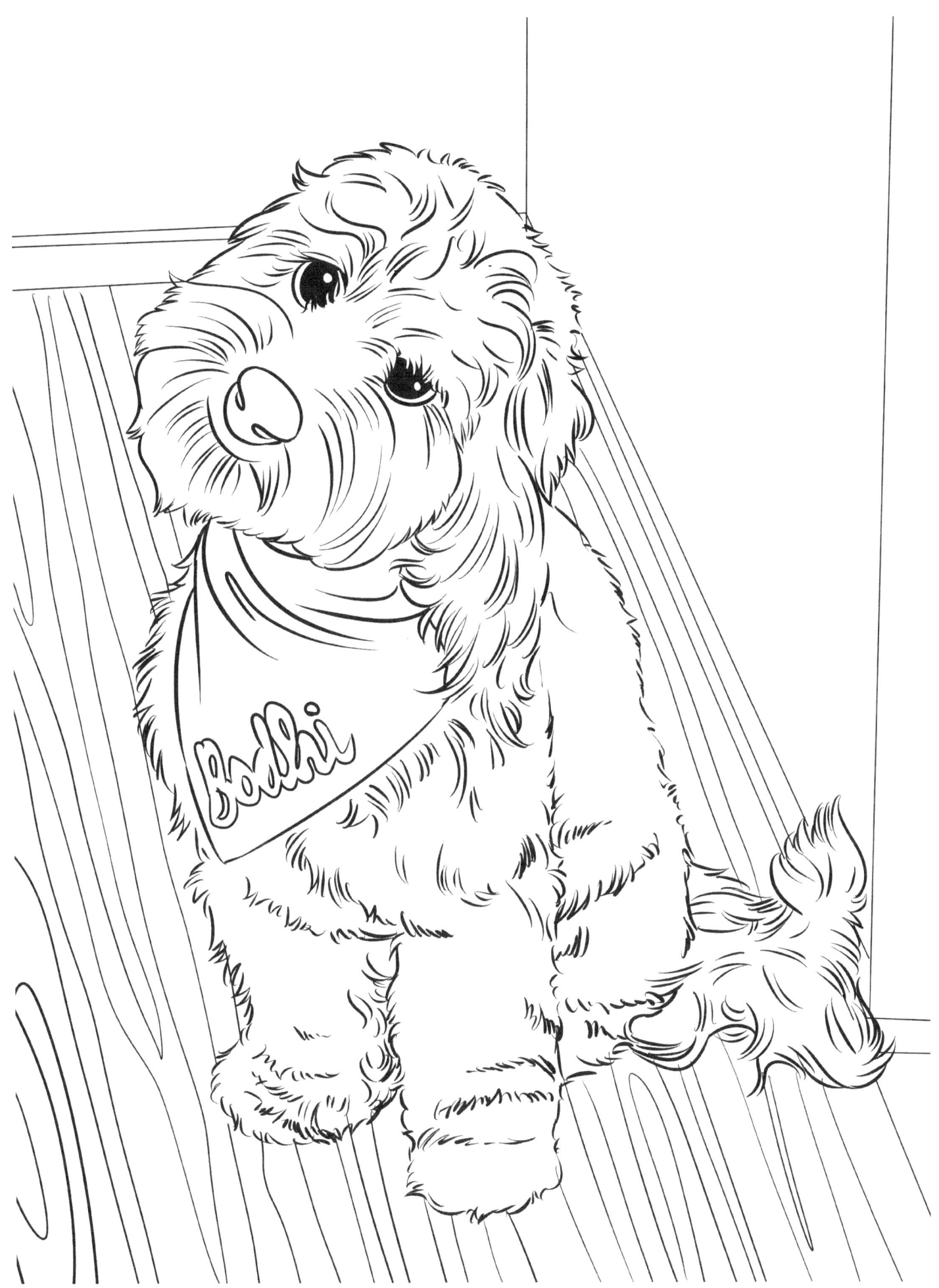

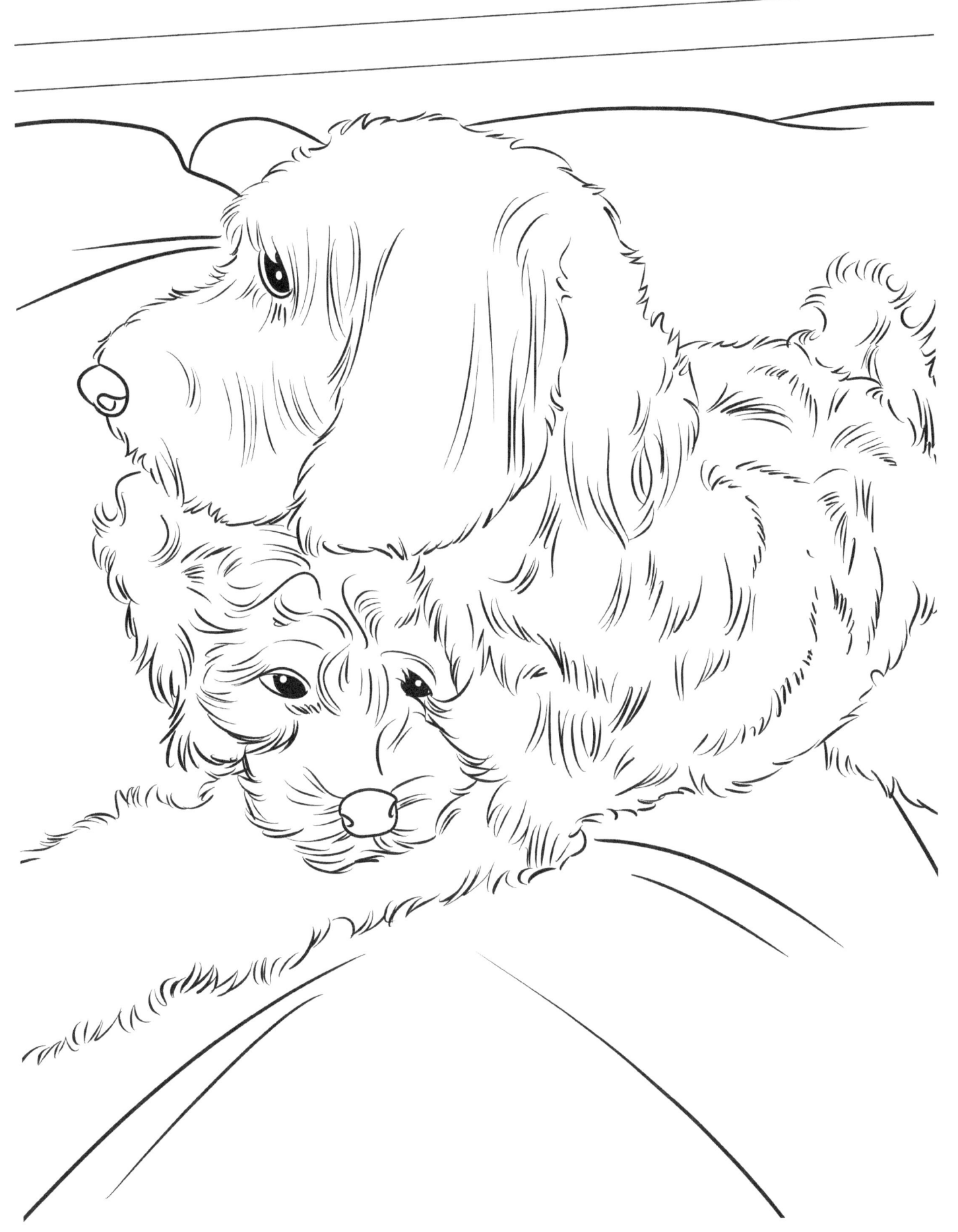

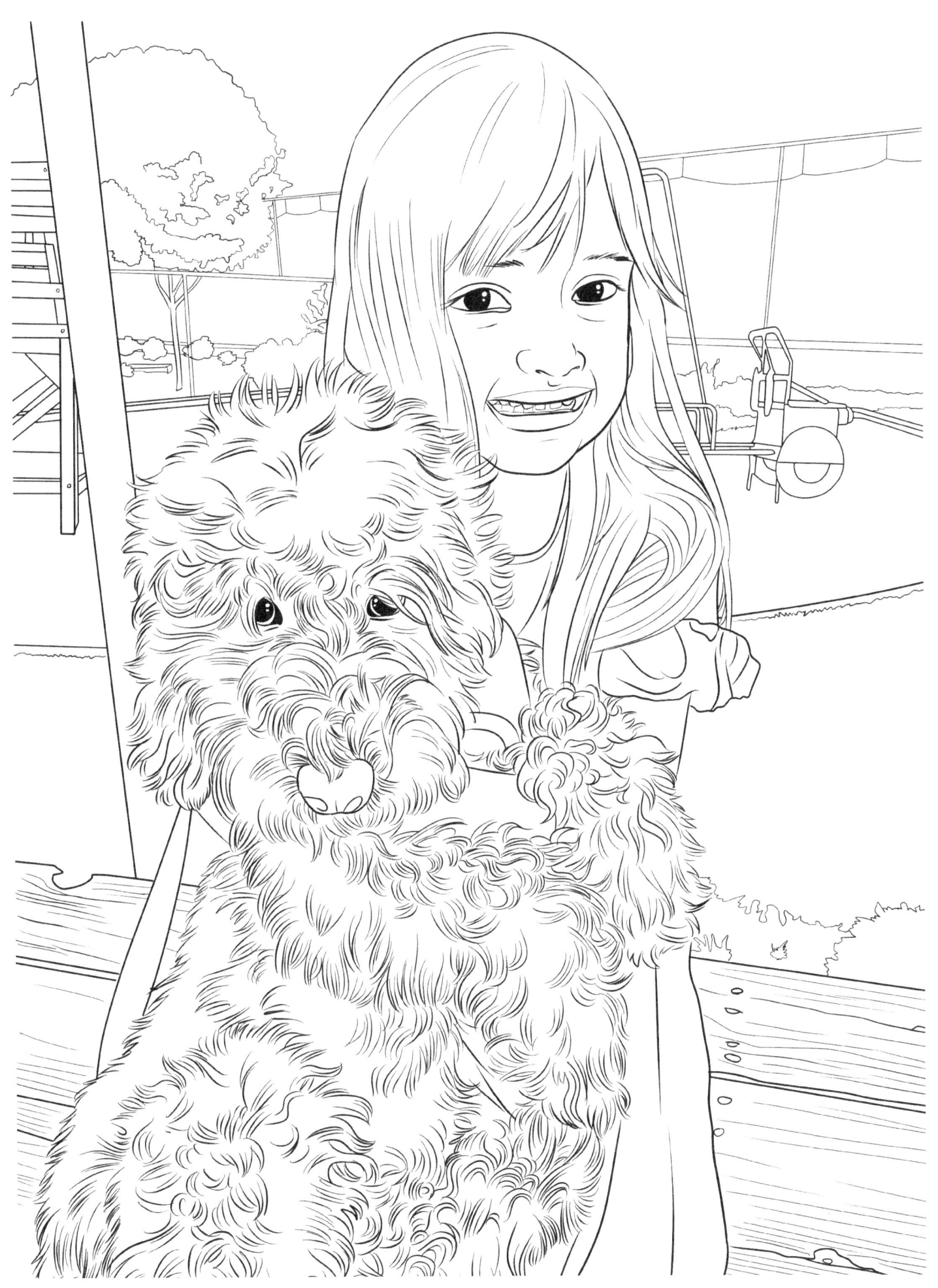

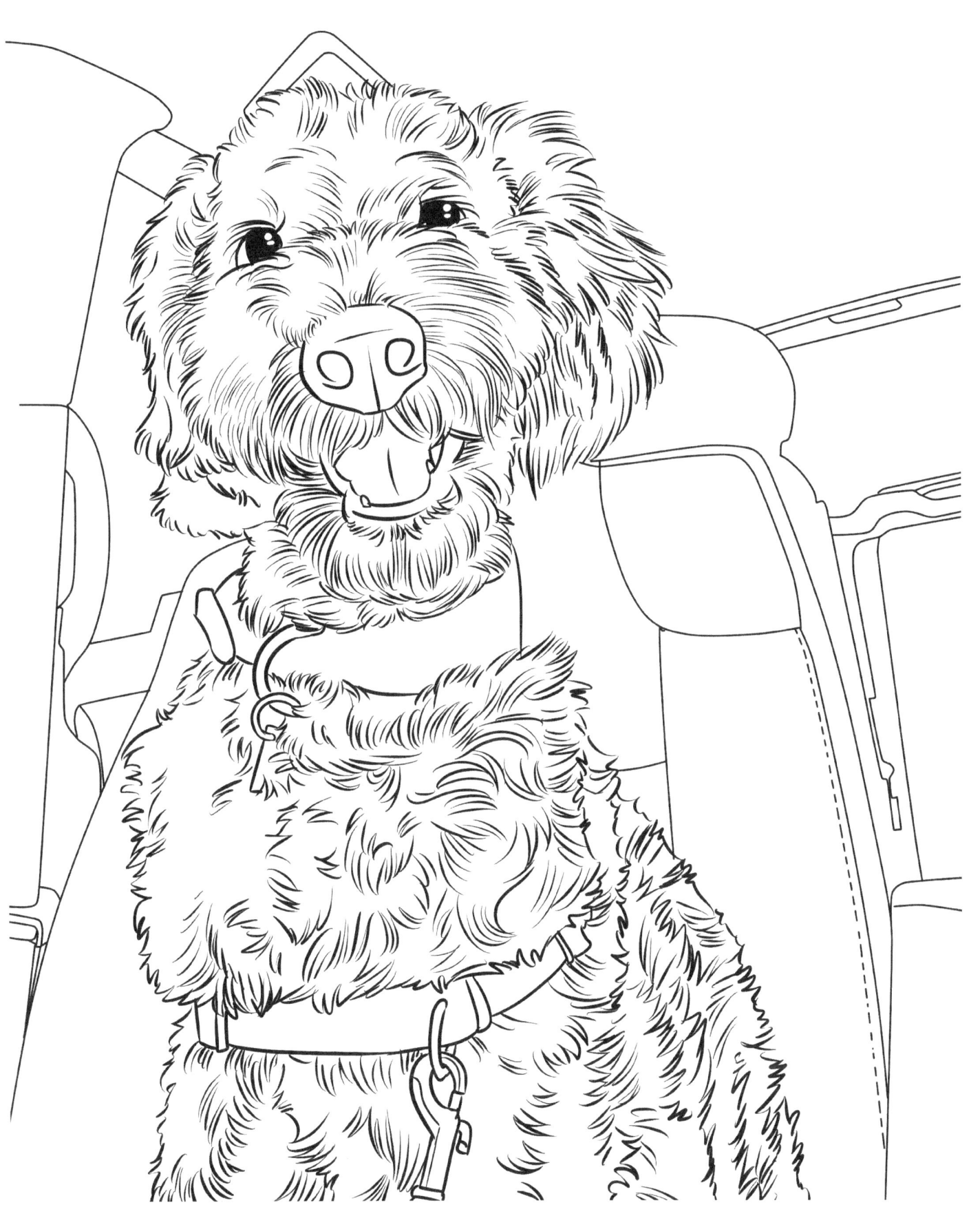

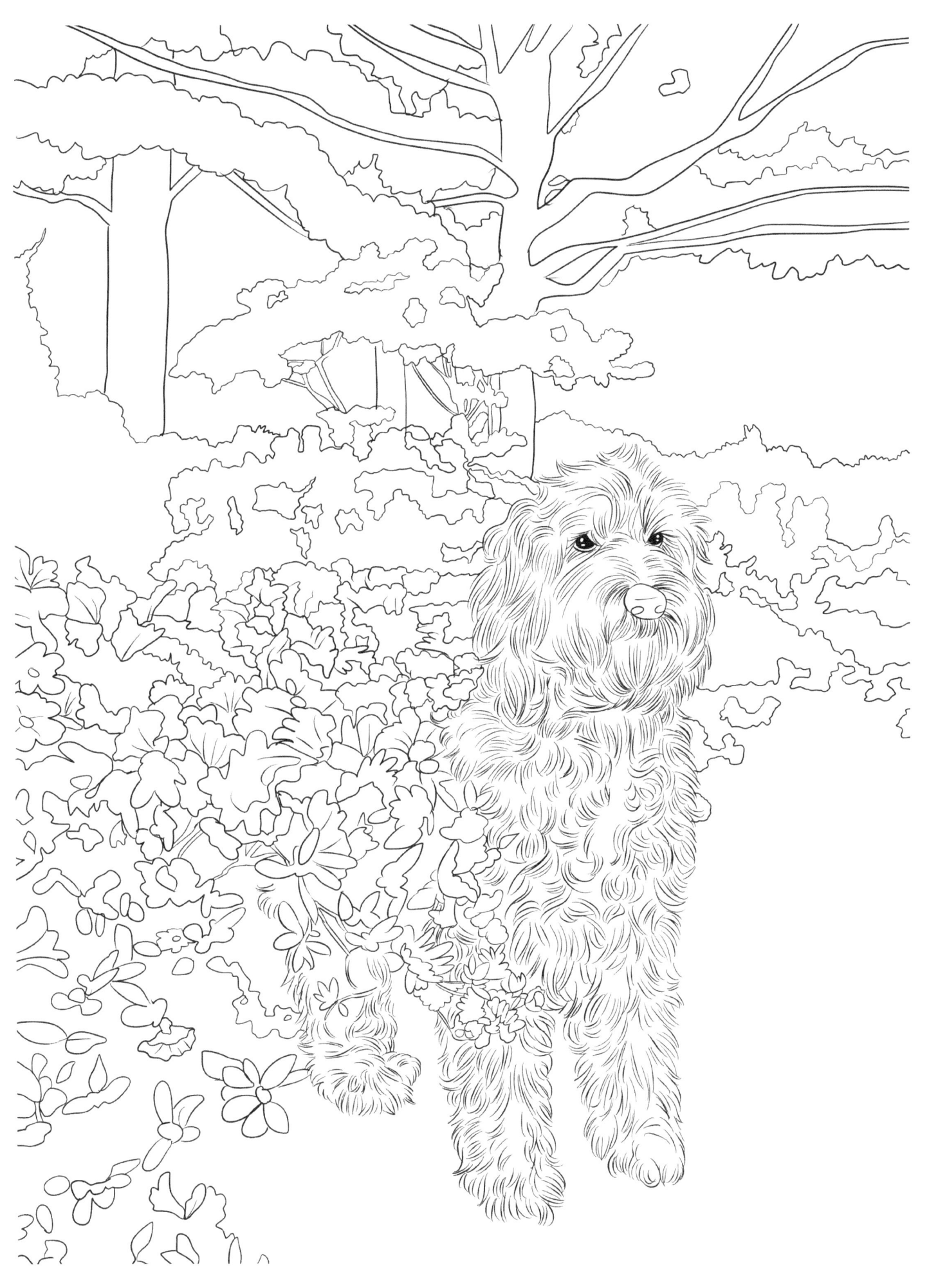

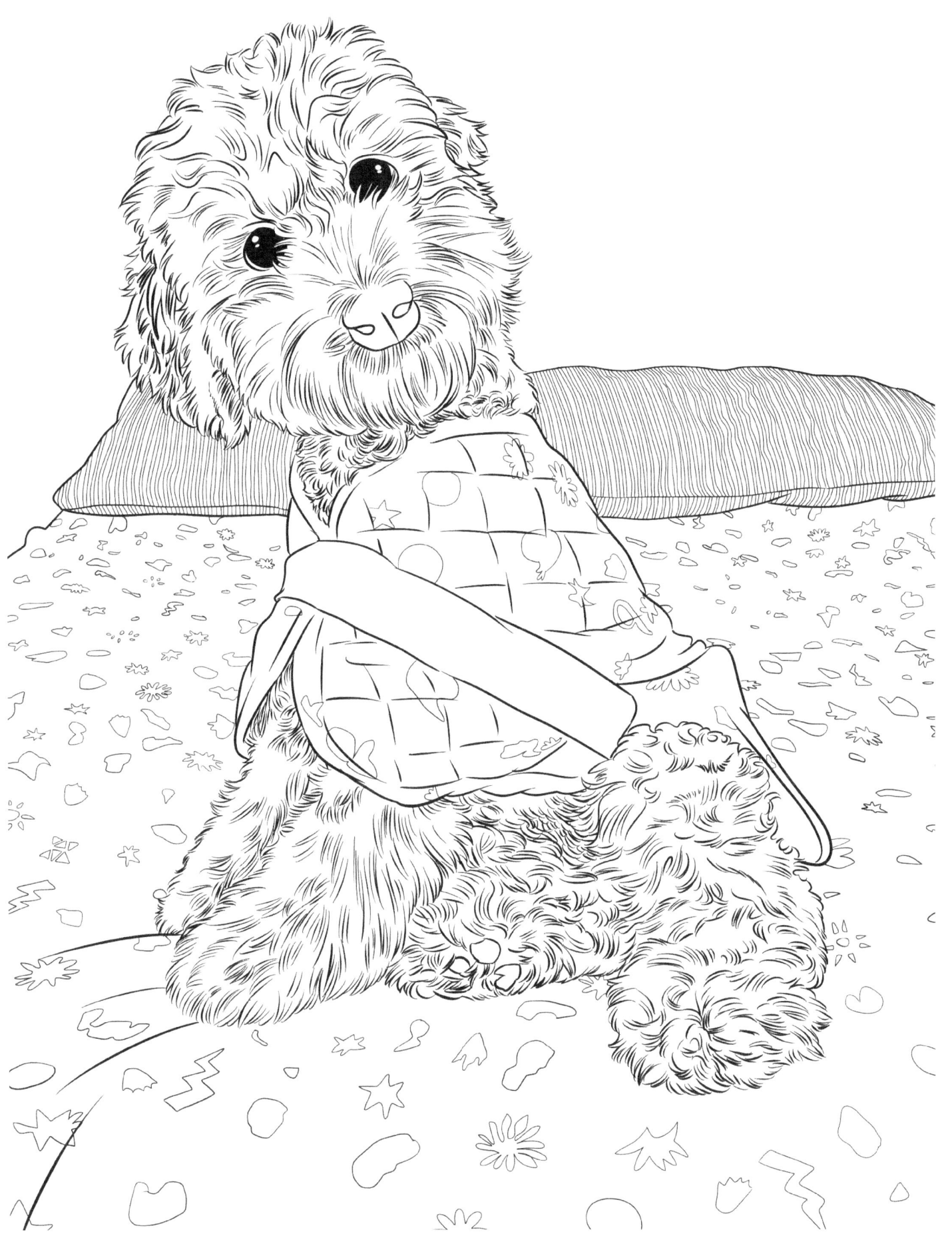

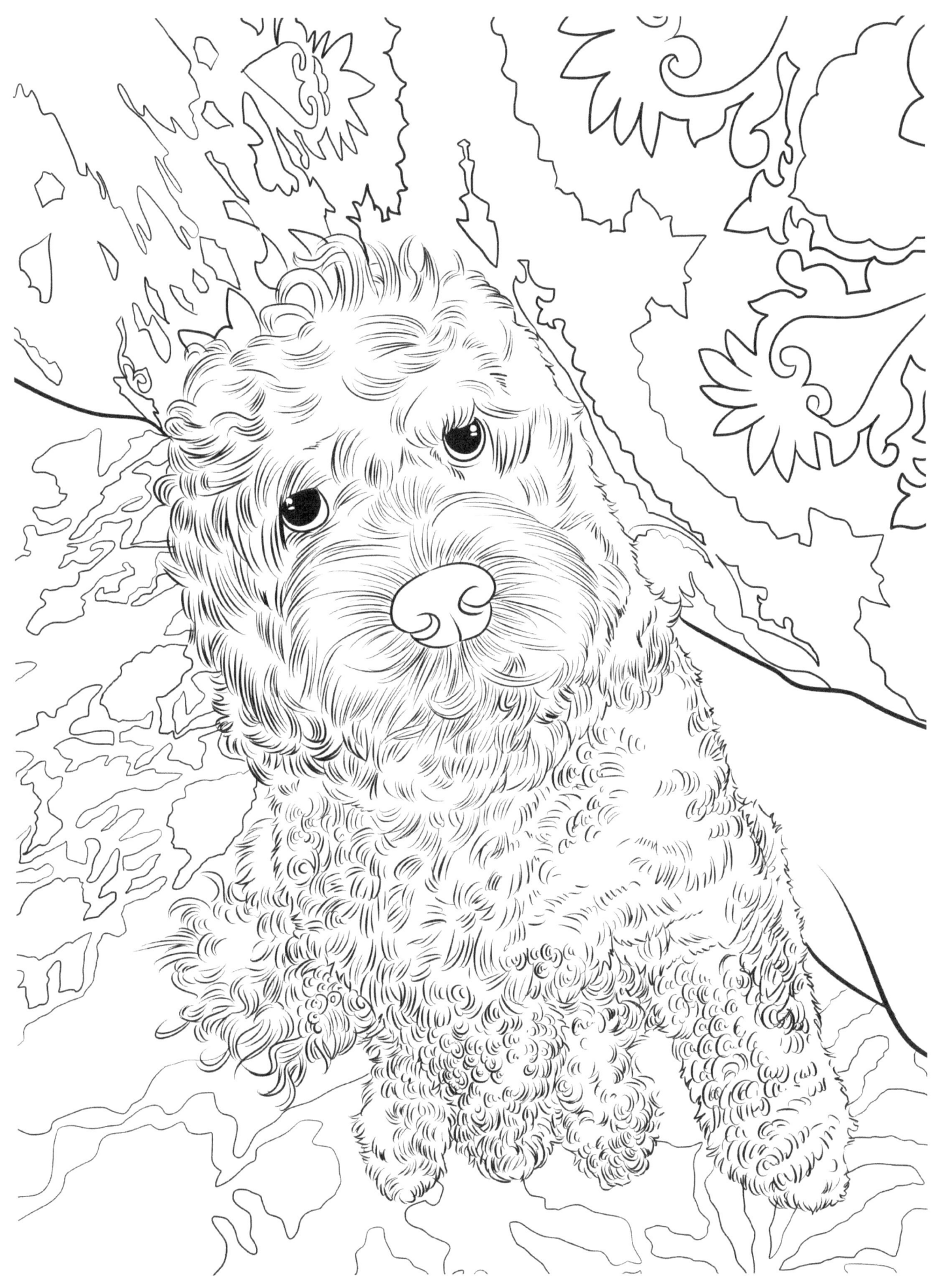

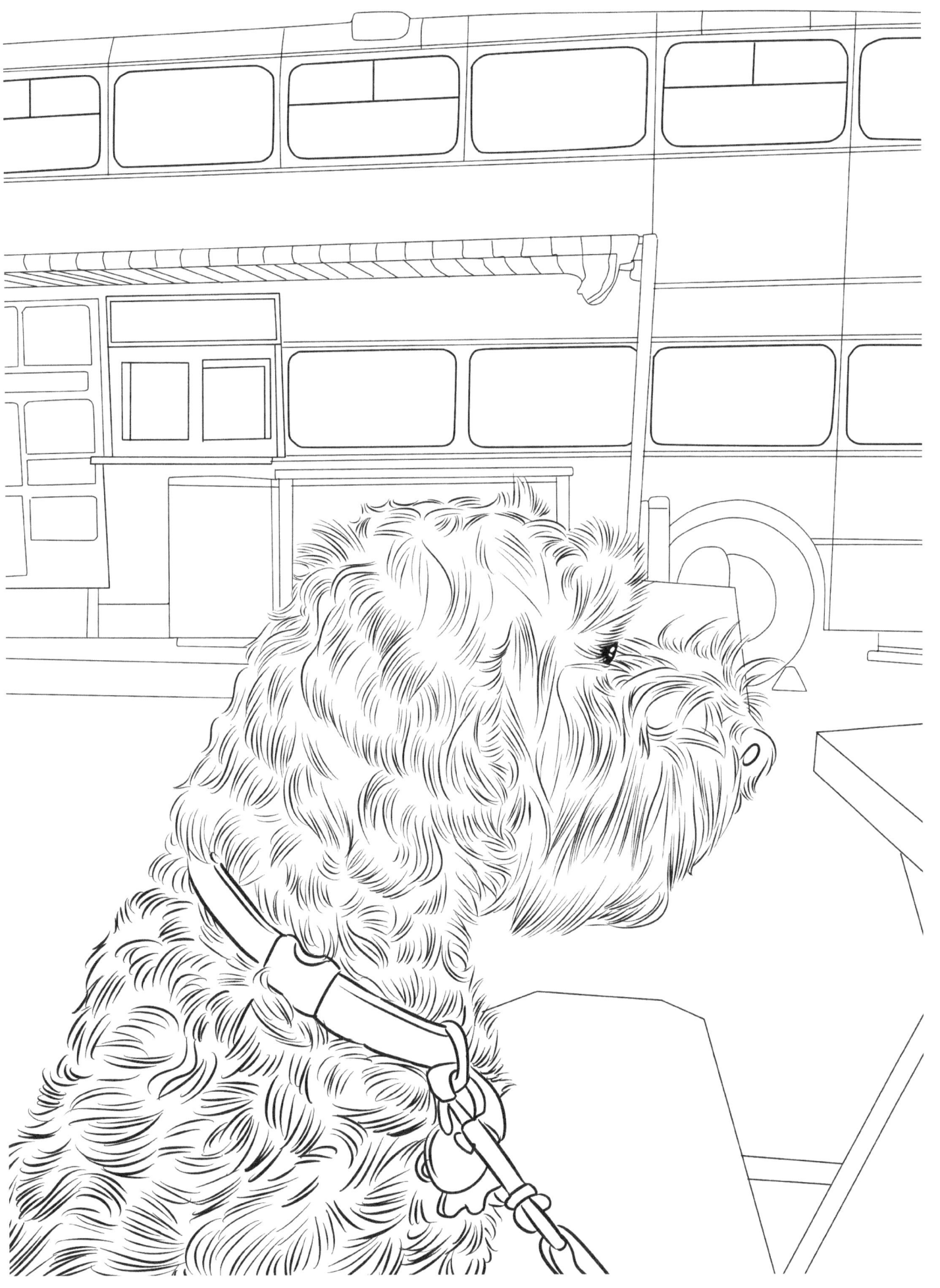

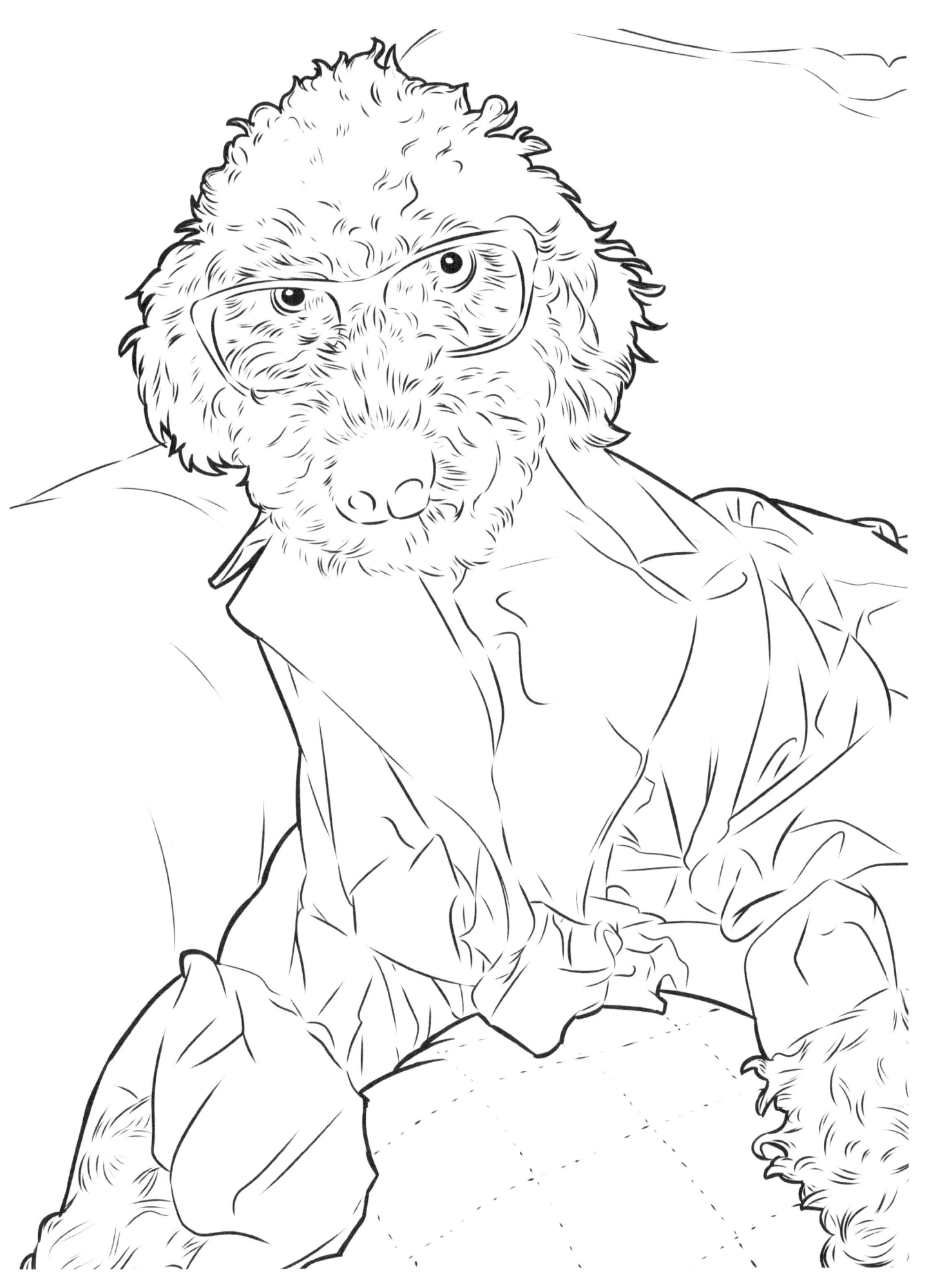

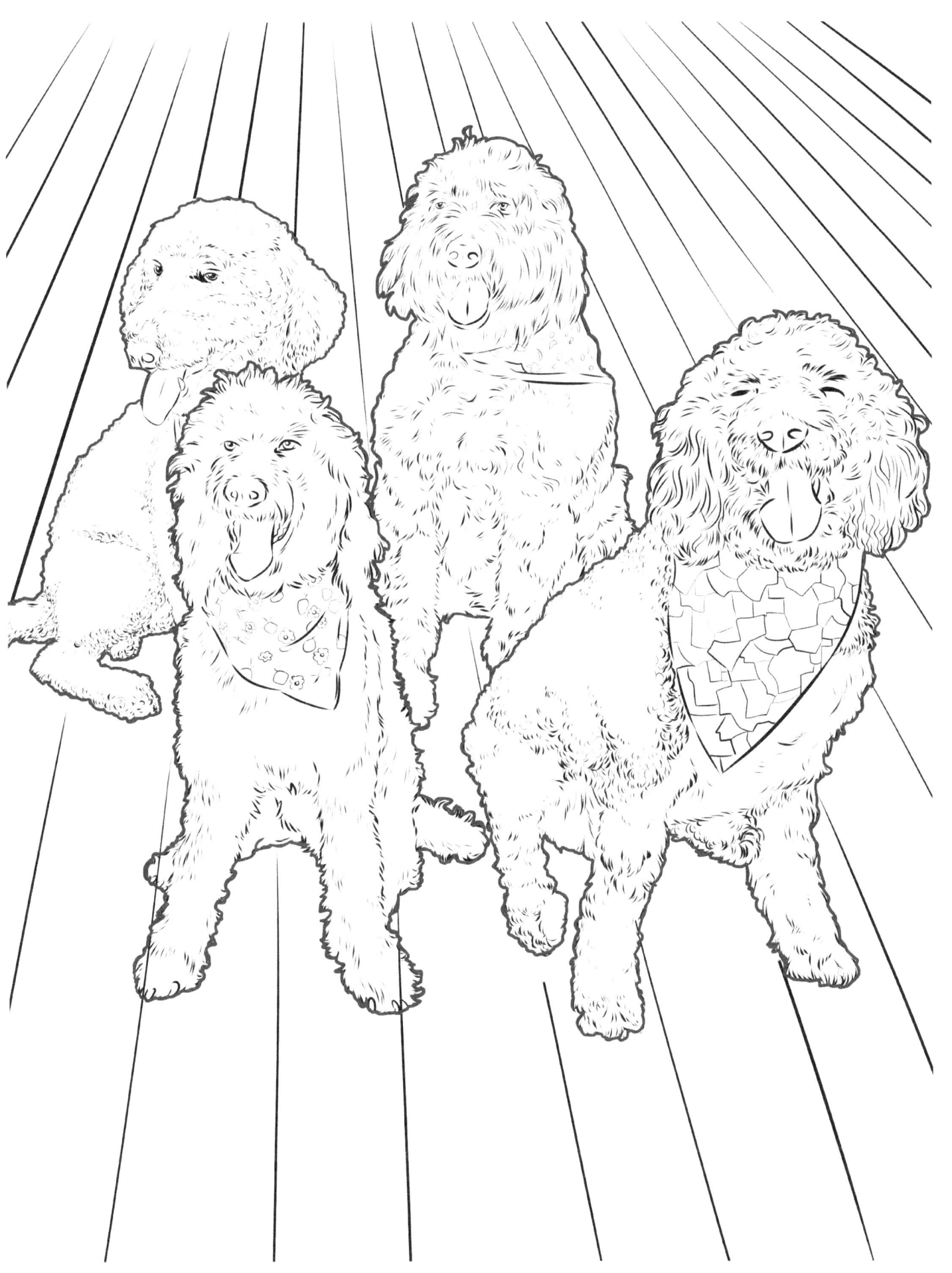

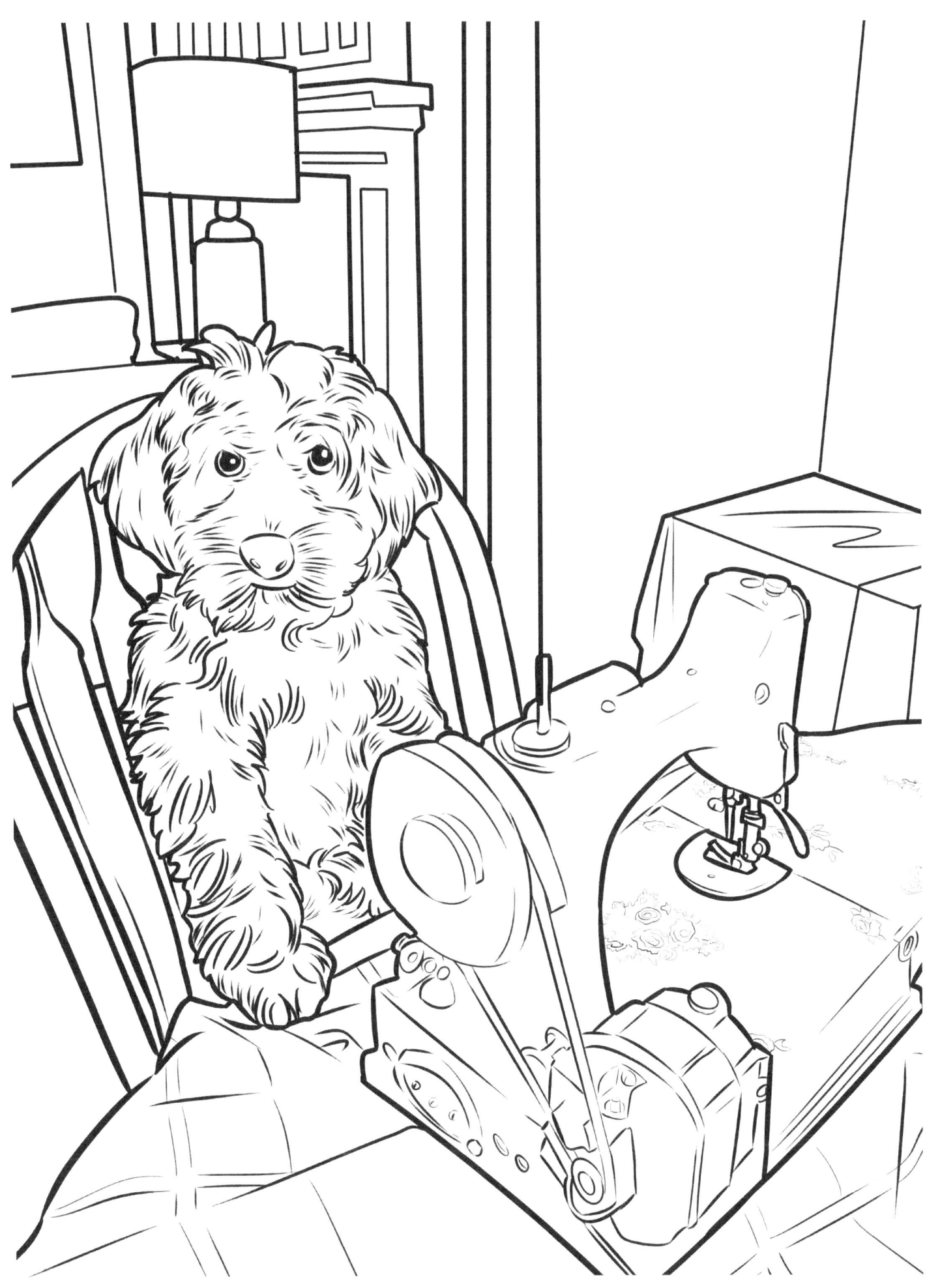

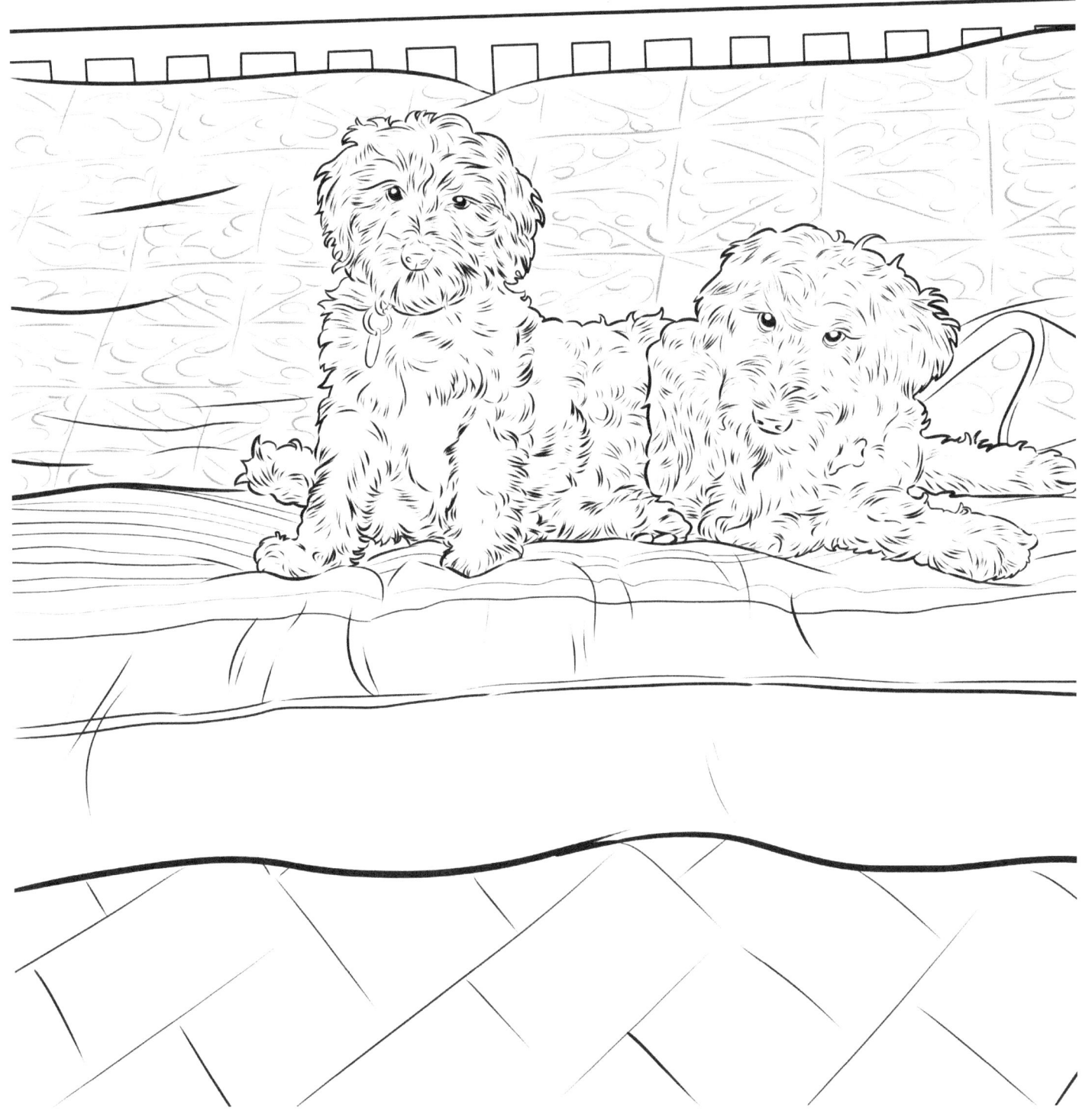

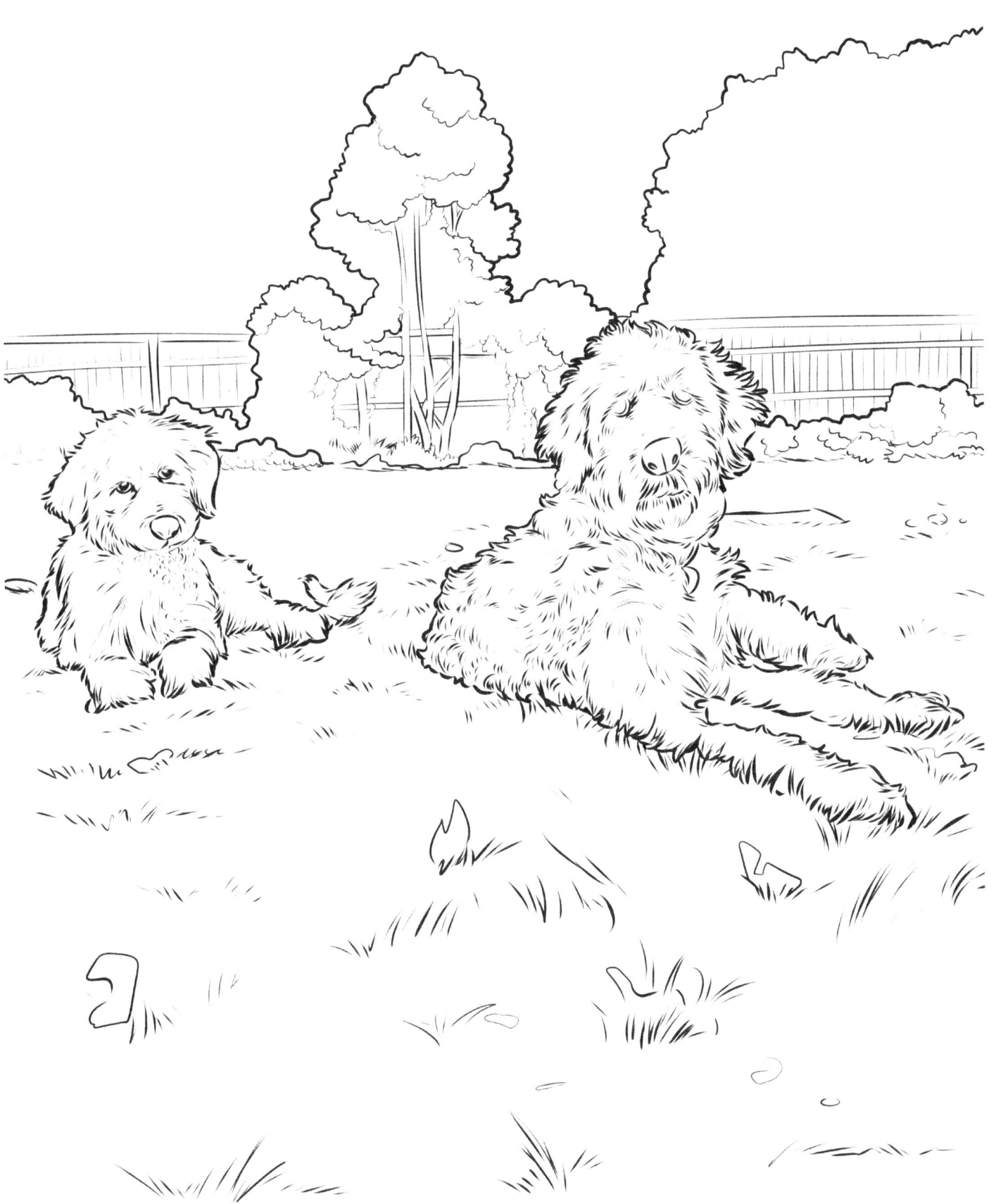

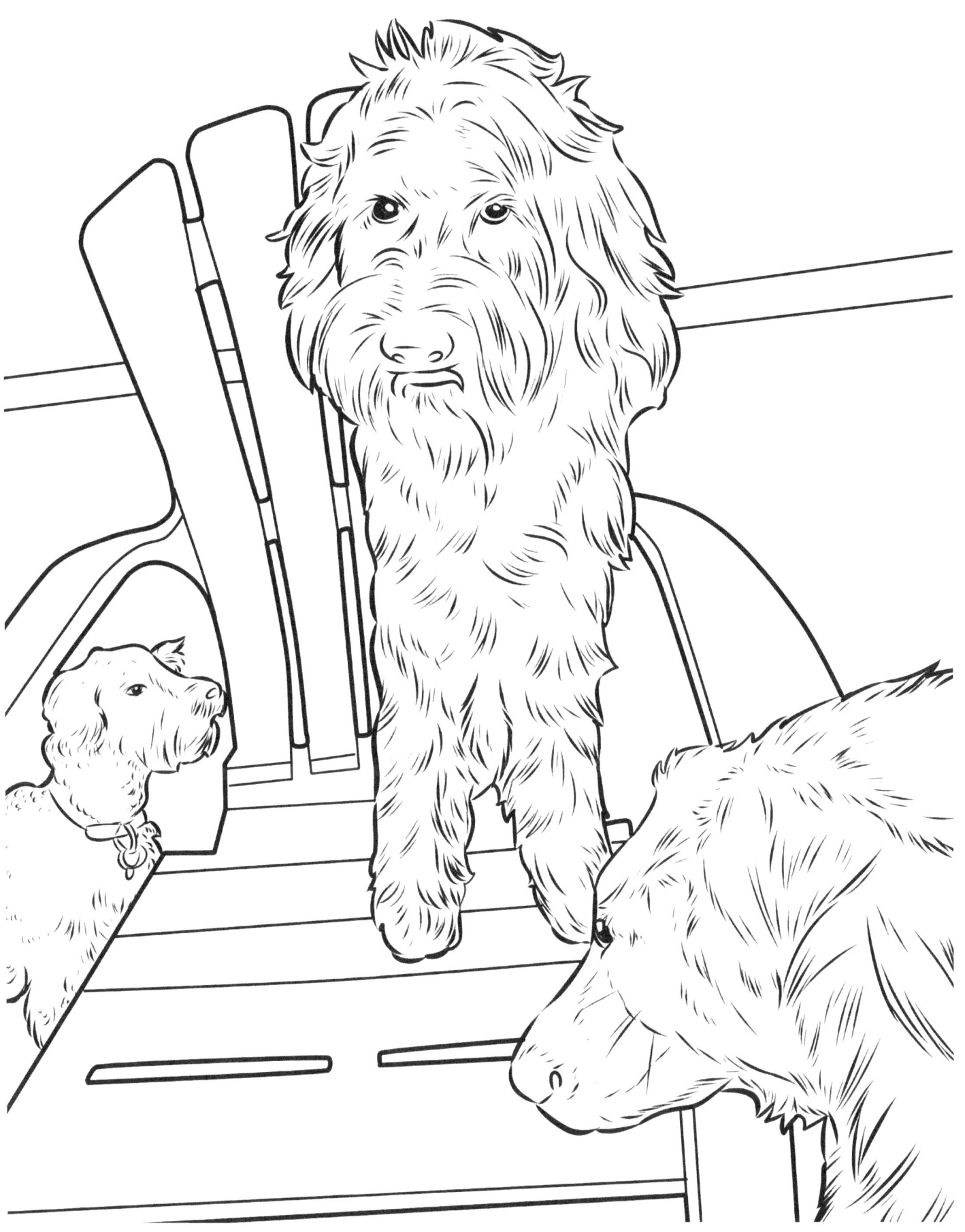

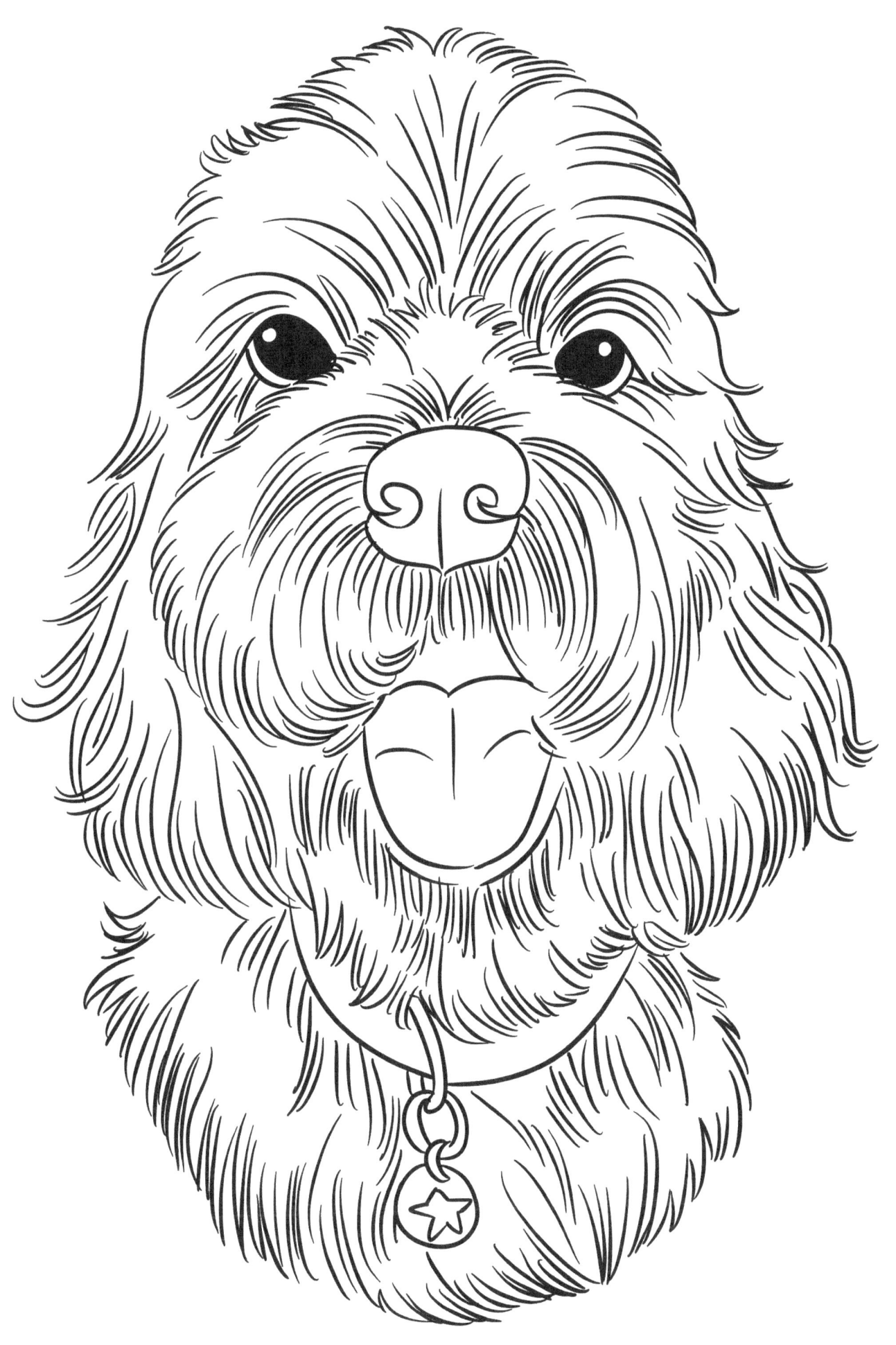

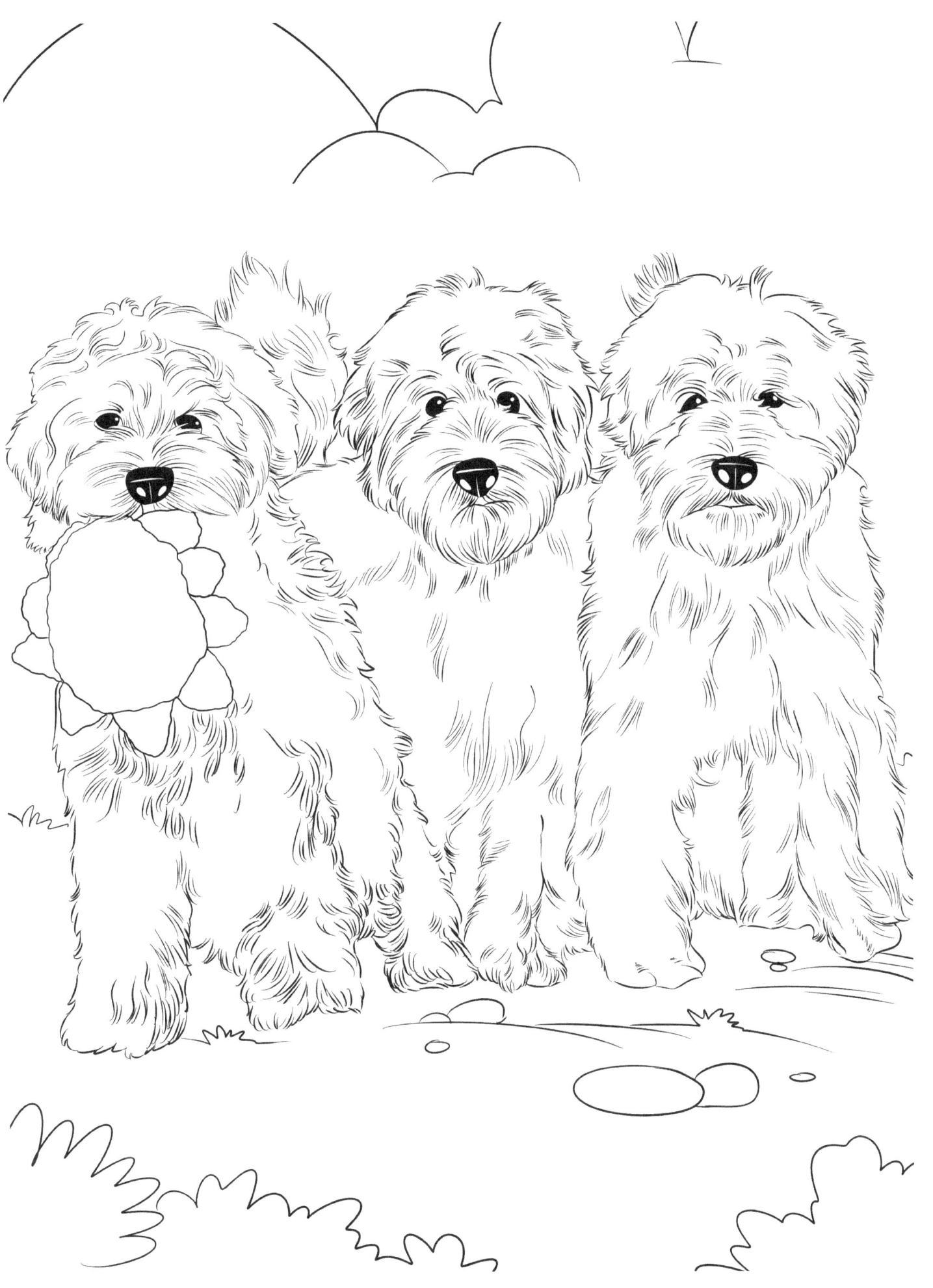

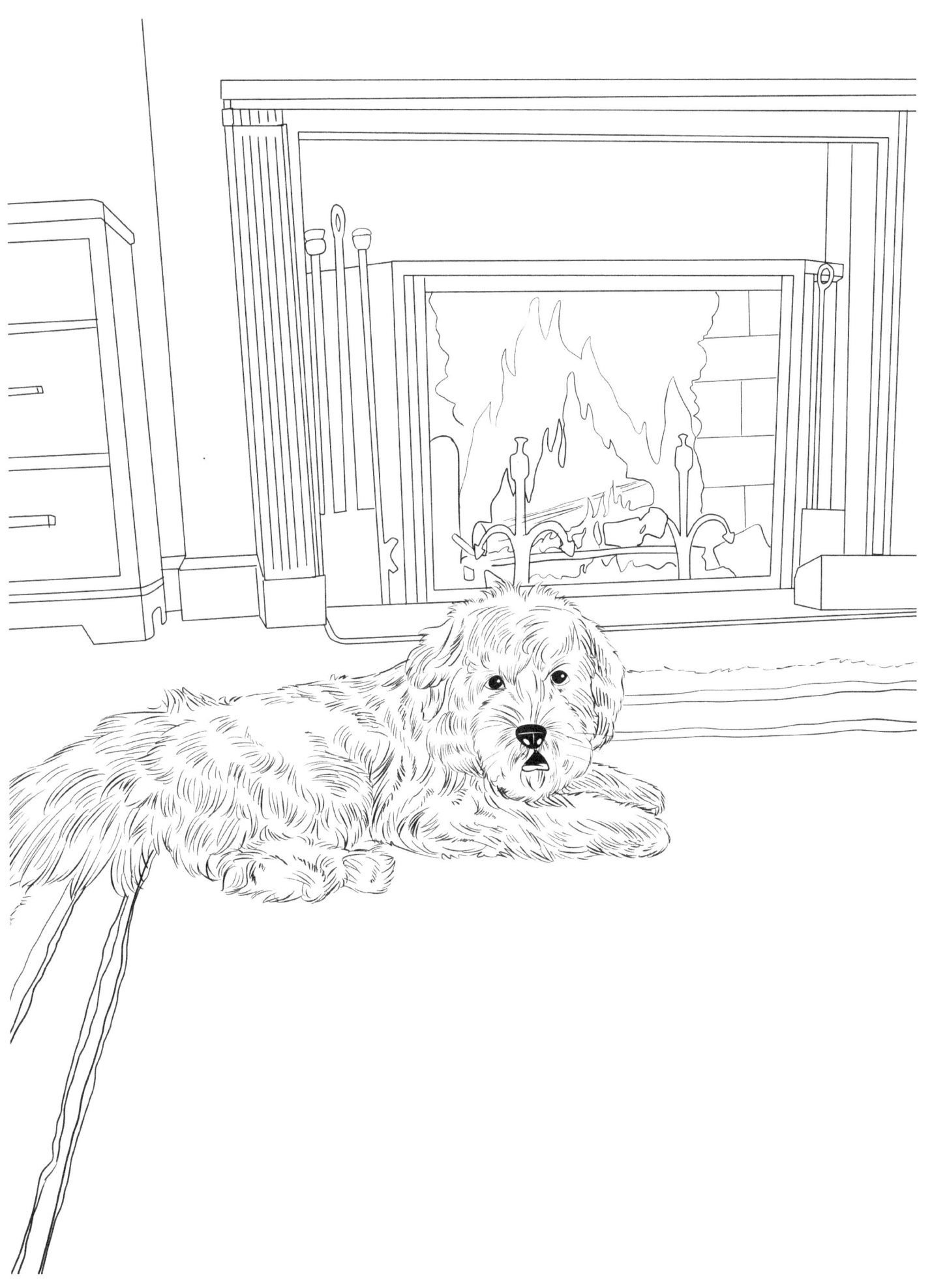

Be sure to visit our website and join our mailing list at:
www.thelittlelabradoodle.com/join

Look for these other great titles from
Little Labradoodle Publishing:

- The Little Labradoodle: Puppy Pickup Day (Picture Book)
- The Little Labradoodle: Puppy Pickup Day (Spanish Picture Book)
- The Little Labradoodle: Puppy Pickup Day (Audio Book)
- The Little Labradoodle: Puppy Pickup Day (Companion Coloring Book)
- The Little Labradoodle Plush
- Doodle Lovers Adult Coloring Book

Coming Soon:

- The Little Labradoodle: Join the KLUB - No Bullies Allowed (Picture Book)

Follow us on social media at:

- TheLittleLabradoodle
- TheLittleLabradoodle
- lil_labradoodle
- TheLittleLabradoodle

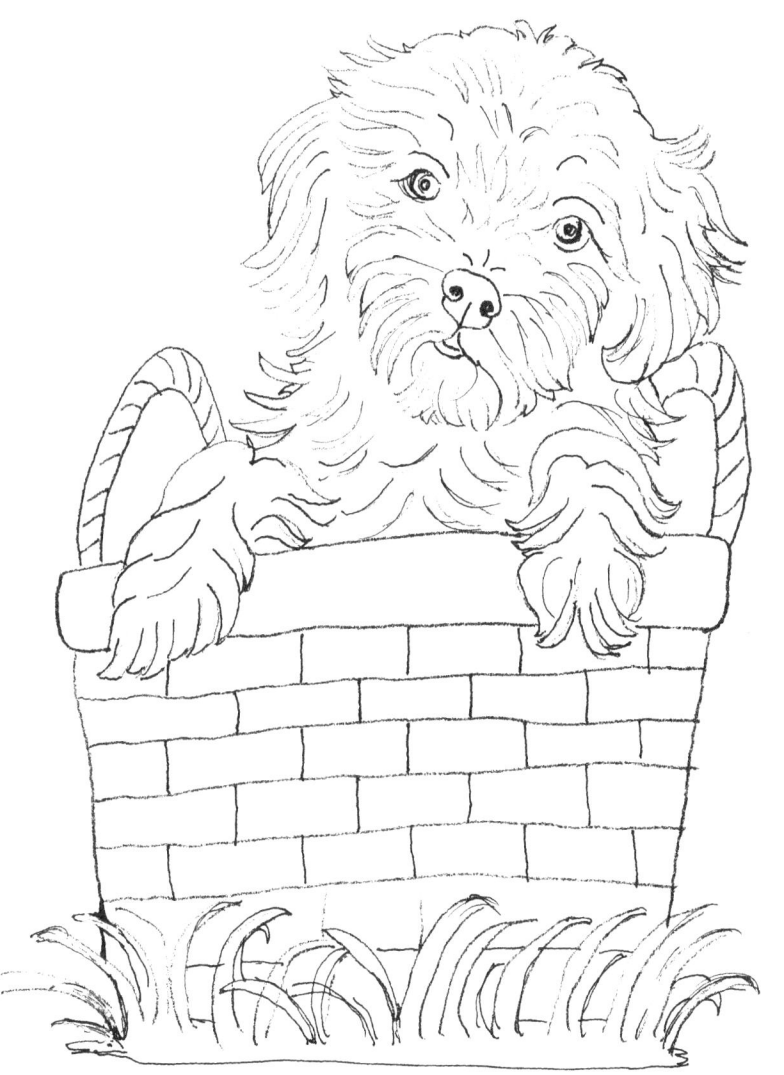

Your FREE Book is Waiting!

Download your copy of the first book in
The Little Labradoodle Series, Puppy Pickup Day at
www.thelittlelabradoodle.com/ppud

Coming Soon

The next book in The Little Labradoodle Series,
Join the KLUB: No Bullies Allowed.

The book will focus on anti-bullying
and empowering kids to make a difference.

Don't forget to join our mailing list and be among
the first to join the KLUB and learn more about
special benefits for members at
www.thelittlelabradoodle.com/join

Help us get the word out.

Please provide a review for this book
to help us get the word out to others.

Your endorsement means so much and helps
us continue to grow and serve others.